OUR TENTH ANNIVERSARY

Many great things have occurred in our lives over the past ten years. However, the birth of the Leelanau Country Inn, and its success, rank right at the top of the list.

This book is a reflection of our 10 years; a way of saying thanks to some of the many staff members, guests and purveyors who have been instrumental in our continued success.

We hope that you will enjoy reading and trying some of our favorite recipes as much as we have enjoyed putting them in this publication, and serving them to you throughout the past 10 years.

-Linda & John Sisson

LEELANAU COUNTRY INN
COOKERY

Leelanau Country Inn Cookery

Food and Wine from the Land of Delight

By Linda & John Sisson

Illustrated by Peggy Core

Edited, with material on wines by Larry Mawby

THE CAIRN PRESS

Suttons Bay, Michigan

The Cairn Press
4519 S. Elm Valley Rd
Suttons Bay, MI 49682

First Edition

Library of Congress Catalog Card Number: 94-71255

Publisher's Cataloging-in-Publication Data
Sisson, Linda, 1952-
Leelanau Country Inn cookery : food and wine from the land of
delight / by Linda & John Sisson ; edited, with material on wines by
Larry Mawby ; illustrations by Peggy Core. - Suttons Bay, Michigan :
The Cairn Press, c1994.
p. : ill. ; cm.
Includes index.
ISBN: 0-9640306-0-8
1. Cookery. 2. Wine Lists. 3. Menus. I. Sisson, John, 1953- II.
Mawby, Larry, 1950- III. Title.
TX715.S57 1994   641.5 dc20

Printed in the United States of America

Title Page illustration by Lyn Boyer-Pennington

Grace...
Come Lord Jesus Be Our Guest
And Let These Gifts to Us Be Blessed.
                                    -Amen.

"Now See Here! ..."

The author of these three words was my grandfather, Ernest K. Baxter. From my earliest days I remember those words coming my way whenever I made a poor judgement. Grandpa used them to instill a simple rule: do things right the first time. They have remained the mortar that binds our actions, forming the structure of quality that together we strive for.

Thanks, Grandpa, we dedicate this to you!

"Nestled in the heart of Leelanau County, an area of Michigan that many call 'Gods Country', is a very special place called the Leelanau Country Inn.
"Full of personality and character, it is evident that owners John & Linda have put a lot of themselves into this 'Dream Come True' which began back in 1984.
"Whether a visitor stops in for a home cooked meal or to spend the weekend, one's expectations are always surpassed. Every special touch and extra detail has been carefully attended to. The high quality standards set by John and Linda are carried out by each member of their team. This is what makes the Leelanau Country Inn unique and truly world class!"

-Paul B. Gordon, Chairman, Gordon Food Service

"It was with great joy that we watched Linda and John take on a labor of love when they opened the Leelanau Country Inn. Linda's charm and John's expertise in the food service business almost guaranteed success. It has been our pleasure to help these two lovely people bring the treasurers of the sea to the land of lakes and forests. It's been a great 10 years, plenty of hard work and worries as with any business but also with well-deserved success."

-Steve Connolly, Chairman and CEO, Steve Connolly Seafood

TABLE OF CONTENTS

Great Beginnings   67

Other Ocean Favorites 135

Poultry & Meat 157

Brunch Favorites 185

PERFECT ENDINGS   209

INDEX   233

AN
EDITOR'S
INTRODUCTION

"In six pages I can't even say 'hello'."
-James Michener

When John and Linda Sisson first asked me about working on this book, John explained that over the years
they'd received many requests for recipes from the guests
of the Inn, and that he and Linda felt that now, on the
10th anniversary of the Inn's opening, they'd like to
celebrate with a book that included a compilation of those
favorite recipes, but that it must be 'more than a recipe
book'. We talked, and talked some more, and now, after
several months and many long hours in the kitchen, at the
computer and the drawing board, this book is 'more than
a recipe book'.

In the book's first chapter, John and Linda welcome you
to their Inn, introduce you to their Kids, let you meet a
few of the many staff members that make your visit to the
Inn pleasant and memorable, tell you about the critical
purveyors who consistently supply the Inn with the
quality foods and other supplies necessary to the proper
functioning of the kitchen, and round out the introduc-
tions with a bit of their own personal history at the Inn.
Reading that chapter will leave no doubt that the people
of the Inn are it's most important asset.

In the chapter titled The Wine List, I've contributed some
information on another important part of the Leelanau
Country Inn experience, the wines produced by Leelanau
Peninsula's four local vintners. Since it first opened, the
Country Inn has featured, to the virtual exclusion of all
other wines, the products of our area's wineries, for which
demonstration of confidence and affection we vintners are
both pleased and proud. In addition to a bit of information about each winery's place in the local scene, and their
wines, the chapter includes a categorization of some wines

and a few principles useful in matching foods and wines. These principles are demonstrated later in the book, as each entree recipe has suggestions for appropriate wines for service with that entree.

Before the recipes commence, a short chapter called Cookery Fundamentals is included. *It is important that even the experienced cook read this before proceeding to the recipes themselves,* as this chapter outlines the basic assumptions we've made about ingredients, equipment and techniques used in the kitchen. The notation system used is explained - of particular import is the Shamrock ☘, signifying that the recipe so marked requires extended preparation time. All of the recipes in this book have been test prepared at the scale given here, and, to the extent possible, the use of specialized kitchen equipment has been avoided. Also, attention has been given to the problem of finding ingredients for home use - in a very few cases, recipes have been altered and test cooked with new, easier to find, ingredients.

In preparing to cook using the recipes in this book, it is vital that good kitchen technique be used. Be aware of the amount of time required to prepare the dish. Read the recipe through, noting where ingredients are themselves the product of other recipes in this book, and prepare those ingredients as required. Assemble all equipment and ingredients before beginning to assemble the dish - trimming cleaning, slicing, dicing, etc as required. Only when everything is laid out ready for use should the actual assembly of the dish begin. You'll find that, where appropriate, the recipes contain hints about cooking techniques used by the professional chef, and that most also include suggested substitutions for ingredients or variations on preparation and service instructions.

As to the eight chapters of recipes themselves, note that the first chapter - Breadings, Stuffings, Sauces & Dressings - is a compendium of recipes, several of which are themselves components that are used in other recipes. You will be referring often to this chapter as you prepare recipes found in later chapters.

Great Beginnings offers a selection of appetizers, some of which might be scaled up and served as entrees, all of which are tasteful starters for a memorable meal. Specific wine suggestions aren't made with the appetizers, in part because I feel that a simple rule applies - always enjoy sparkling wines with appetizers at the beginning of the meal, frequently continue with a sparkler during the meal, and generally conclude the meal by sipping a bit of sparkling wine with dessert.

Soups, Salads & Side Dishes contains a group of recipes that fill out the menu, providing a complement to the showcase entree, and a bridge between the appetizer and the main course. When served with selections from Great Beginnings, these dishes make nice luncheon meals.

Then it's on to the three entree chapters: Lake & Ocean Fish, Other Ocean Favorites, and Poultry & Meat. As you look over entree recipes, note that in most cases they've been scaled to serve 4 to 6 people. Generally, this was a scale UP from the Inn's practice of individual entree preparation. Also, several possible substitutes are given for the main ingredient, making each recipe a mini-cookbook in itself. Note also that each entree recipe includes a suggested dinner menu composed of other recipes in the book - useful meal planning advice. Also, in these three chapters, wine service suggestions are given for each entree.

The chapter called Brunch Favorites contains recipes for somewhat larger groups. These are the dishes found at the Inn's Sunday Brunch, and have been scaled for your use in entertaining, as they are fairly easy to prepare and they retain their appearance and flavor for a relatively long time while being kept warm in a serving dish. The recipes in this chapter, coupled with Great Beginnings and Perfect Endings, are the menu for a perfect party.

And the final chapter, Perfect Endings, closes the recipes with a selection of the indulgent favorites we've enjoyed for years at the Inn.

To help you find your way through the book, in addition to the Table of Contents where all recipes are listed, an Index is provided that lists each occurrence of each recipe. Useful, for example, if you really want to try a particular recipe and want to find every suggested menu that calls for that dish, or to see if it's used as a component of another recipe. Also indexed are major ingredients, whether called for in the recipe's ingredient list or in Variations. This should be useful if, for example, you've just gotten some fresh Whitefish, and want to find every recipe that might be prepared using Whitefish.

Throughout the book, the pen and ink drawings by Peggy Core serve to beautify the page; clarify complex instructions; amuse; illustrate ingredients, tools, kids; remind us always that cookery, a domestic art, is, when well done, a nourisher of the spirit as well as the body, and thus a higher art; and work to make this book 'more than a recipe book'.

Lastly, before it's too late, before you go off into the book, let me say hello.

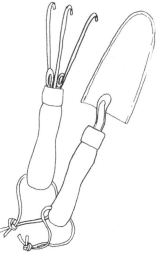

"Knowledge is like a garden:
if it is not cultivated,
it cannot be harvested."
-Folk lore from Guinea

WELCOME TO THE COUNTRY INN

"He goes not out of his way
that goes to a good inn."
-George Herbert

Those of you learning about the Inn and its innkeepers for the first time should be introduced to the 'stars' of the operation; the Sisson kids, Sambucca Anne, Whitney Elizabeth and Ditto Lee. Quite naturally, we are very proud of our kids and their accomplishments.

Sambucca, the eldest, is now thirteen years old. Since Linda and I were married on September 12, 1981 and welcomed Sambucca to the family on September 14th, it should be pointed out that Sambucca and her 'sisters' come equipped with four legs each and tails that won't stop wagging.

A forlorn and abandoned puppy, adopted from the Petoskey Humane Society, Sambucca has graced the Sisson home with loyalty and love. She has been a prominent fixture of the Inn since its opening, roaming the grounds and, on request, making personal appearances in the restaurant itself.

Her picture, proudly presented next to the host stand, elicited the information from several guests that she is a Bearded Collie. When she became seriously ill during her ninth year, her 'pediatrician', Dr. Dan Aja, owner of Cherry Bend Animal Hospital, suggested that a companion might help her regain her health. Thus the arrival of Whitney Elizabeth, a six week old AKC registered Bearded Collie, who became a close friend and the inspiration Sambucca needed to get back on her feet.

Now comes Ditto Lee, a bouncy Bichon Frise, named for her hero, Rush Limbaugh, and an 'aunt', Joni Lee. Ditto joined the flock in January 1992. Her assignment - give

Sambucca a little rest from the super-energized (a Bearded Collie trait) attention she was receiving from Whitney Elizabeth. It worked. After a couple of days Whitney and Ditto were inseparable and Sambucca, while still probably fondly remembering the good old days when she was an only 'child', is able to enjoy her golden years in comparative peace. At least until Moira Lyn arrives.

What love and companionship! The world of the Beardies and Bichons!

The success of the Inn over the past ten years lies mainly in the fact that we have surrounded ourselves with some of the finest professionals in the business. We are truly proud of the members of the team and the work they do to insure the total satisfaction of our guests. The restaurant business is notorious for staff turnover. What is truly remarkable and an exception in this day and age is having members of a staff stay in one place for a decade. We have been blessed by more than a handful of exceptions.

Stephanie Tietje is a ten year veteran of numerous positions, and our (soon to be attorney) niece. Steph has grown in so many ways over the years. From that sweet little girl helping as a buser, to a short tenure as a server and then settling in as night hostess and reservationist during the day. Steph graduated from Leland High School, Valedictorian. Went on to graduate with honors from Hillsdale College, and now is in her first year of law school at Wake Forest.

Chris Tietje, another ten year veteran of the dish room and the salad prep area, is now a lead cook on the line. All this, and he has yet to celebrate his eighteenth birthday. As Tietje is not the most common name, you probably have guessed by now he is our nephew. Although nepotism got him the job at age eight, skill, hard work and growth in all facets of life is what has kept it. At this rate he can retire (20 & out) at the ripe old age of twenty eight.

Wendy Jo Aylsworth - You may know her as Wendy Jo, maybe, Wendy, or Jo or even Helen. Whatever name she is using at the time, you have a true gem in your presence. Jo was in the very first training class back in May, 1984. She has worked at the Inn ever since and for the past few years has assumed the responsibility of Head Waitress. Jo's strength in service and ability to handle pressure under most any situation has made her a very valuable part of the team. But take away the service strength and every other skill she offers and you are still left with one super person. She received the first Employee of the Year award the Inn issued and is, in our book, the Employee of the Decade.

Lou Bufka - Officially Maintenance Supervisor, however, there are few hats he hasn't worn over the past ten years. Lou, referred by me as 'my son' has proven to be one of the most honorable, trustworthy, loyal, and dedicated people we have ever known. Lou has been, and is today, involved in almost every aspect of the day to day operations. The attributes listed above have been appreciated by us more than words could say. No one knows what the future brings for any of us. But as far as the 'Kids', Linda and I are concerned, we hope it has Lou in it with us.

Matt Hill is one of the first individuals hired in May of 1984. Then a salad-dish employee, Matt soon elevated himself to a line cook through his skill and work ethic. A tough young man who knew the difference between right and wrong, and could distinguish between good and poor quality. Tell him once the way it should be done and you don't ever have to worry about it again. Matt left the Inn to pursue a four year commitment to the U. S. Marine

"Being a more metropolitan type, my pilgrimage north in 1984, to attend the grand opening of the Leelanau Country Inn was a bewildering experience and my first exposure to a Country Inn. Out in the middle of nowhere, I approached this grand structure. Intuitively, I knew this would be a successful venture.

"I was also fortunate to be able to be a guest in 1989 for the Inn's fifth anniversary party and now consider it my escape from my citified life. All my restaurant visits are now compared to the superior cuisine and service of the Inn and few live up to their standards."

-Peggy Mensch

Corps. After discharge, he returned to the Inn and took over the position he had earned years before, Kitchen Manager. Under his leadership the high standards of quality established from our first day have been at least maintained and where needed, improved. He was and is a key element of our success and a valuable member of our management team.

Jeanne Foglesong, a nine year veteran, and Sue Murphy, eight years and counting, round out our 'exceptions' club. Jeanne is unflappable under pressure and a true joy to be around. Sue has been a spot of sunshine since the day she arrived. As an extra treat we have been able to watch her daughter, Cady, grow into quite a young lady.

We have had literally hundreds of special people grace our property over these ten years. There is no way to honor all of them by listing their names. Many of our staff regulars join us just for the summer months during their education process. Depending upon at what position and age they started, many were with us for four or five years. Our sincere thanks to them all for their contributions in the past and thanks, too, to the staff that stands ready to serve you today and tomorrow.

At the Leelanau Country Inn we've always sought the best quality fresh fish and seafood, and we've never been disappointed by the products of Steve Connolly Seafood of Boston, Massachusetts, our sole supplier of the fresh ocean fish and other seafood we serve at the Inn.

In 1941, Steve Connolly, fresh out of the High School of Commerce, got his first job in the seafood industry. Except for a hitch in the U. S. Navy during World War Two and studies at Boston University, he spent the next 37 years working his way up from billing clerk to fish

"Through the years we have had many pleasurable dining experiences at the Inn. The Casciano family has celebrated many birthdays, Anniversaries, Mother's Day brunches or the two of us for just a quiet evening out. Thanks to all the staff for the great food, friendly service and our personalized menus for the occasions. Our sincere congratulations go to you, John & Linda for the past ten years."
 -Mr. & Mrs. Dan Casciano Jr.

buyer to sales manager to vice-president and general manager of a large, successful Boston seafood house.

At age 53 he decided to go out on his own and follow his dreams. He wanted to found a company which was more responsive to the needs of its customers and employees as well. He adopted the logo of a ship's helm with the slogan, "Steer A Course To Quality."

Quality has been the mainstay of Steve's life. Quality products, quality employees, and quality customers; a program which has worked well. In just a few years he opened five state of the art plants; three in Boston, one in Gloucester at the head of the harbor, and one in Nantucket. He strategically located these plants to take full advantage of the geographical supply of fish. He consistently buys "Top of the Trip" because he is there when the boats land their catch. Steve has scoured the world to gather the finest exotic species for his customers. He went to Rungis in Paris, Oahu and Kona in Hawaii, Tsukiji Market in Tokyo, Halifax and Yarmouth in Canada, Prince Edward Island and just returned from Australia. These are just a few of his travels in search of the finest quality products both at home and abroad; travels too numerous to list here. If it swims and is great eating, Steve is committed to handling the product. As one who has dealt exclusively with Steve for over 25 years I can speak to the fact that his customers truly appreciate the great variety he serves as well as the wonderful quality. Three years ago Steve established his own in-house microbiology laboratory in order to give his customers the comfort level they deserve. You can be sure his fish are truly Pure Fresh™.

From 1985 to 1987 Steve was president of the New England Fish Processors Cooperative. With E. P. A. approval, he ran a barge out of Gloucester to dispose of fish waste 12 miles at sea. He literally kept the entire fish industry in Massachusetts in business. Without the barge, the industry would have been deluged in fish frames.

In 1990 Steve was chosen Small Business Person of the Year for Massachusetts, Purveyor of the Year by the ACF Chefs de Cuisine, Purveyor of the Year by Les Amis d'Escoffier Club and a finalist in the Entrepreneur of the Year Awards. In 1993 he was a winner of the Blue Chip Initiative Award of the U. S. Chamber of Commerce.

Steve's business acumen is well documented. Starting his 53rd year in the business he loves, Steve is looking forward to serving his many friends for many more years to come.

There are so many food service companies for a restauranteur to deal with, trying to secure business by promising the moon, that it is difficult for an operator to please them all by giving each a piece of the pie. When you can deal with one company that offers the services and product line that you need to be successful, you are really blessed.

We are blessed! Meet Gordon Food Service. GFS is and has been a family owned business for many decades. From Paul Gordon as Chairman, John Gordon as Secretary/Treasurer, and Dan Gordon as President, the company is committed to the family name and reputation. Everyone connected with GFS has the same family bond. I would like to share their Company Philosophy with you:

"Our Philosophy is simple:

"ON CHANGE: We believe that change is a way of life; we should welcome it, we should look forward to it; we should create and force change, we should not wait to react to change created by others.

"ON GROWTH: We believe in controlled permanent growth for both the company and the individual. We will only grow as a company if we grow individually. Further, we believe that each person's contribution is meaningful and that each person helping us grow is entitled to share in such growth through sharing in company profits and meaningful individual incentive based on individual performance

"ON BUSINESS CONDUCT: We believe in complete integrity with each other, our customers, our suppliers and our community. Most important is the complete openness of information, and the ability for everyone to accept constructive ideas from each other.

"ON THE RACE OF LIFE: We believe that to be complete people we must succeed and not fail; we must not drift aimlessly and without purpose; that the race will indeed be won by the swift. Accordingly, each of us, and therefore our company, must be among the swift.

"FINALLY: We Believe in God, who sent his son, Jesus Christ, to earth to show us himself, and for us to be complete people, we must accept him by faith."

I suppose all companies have a stated philosophy, whether in print or not. A key difference with Gordon Food Service is that they practice their philosophy as a way of life. When you can deal with a company like this, why look elsewhere? We don't.

Linda and I, while still relatively young, find ourselves celebrating fifty combined years in the restaurant business and ten years as owners of the Leelanau Country Inn.

"It has been our good fortune to have discovered the Leelanau Country Inn ten years ago. So many good memories have been shared by your wonderful staff with our whole family and all our friends.
"Our congratulations to John & Linda for making the Inn the "Jewel of the North" with your outstanding food and warm hospitality!
"Many more years of happiness, health and success!"
                    -Mr. & Mrs. Al Jones

I actually got my start in the food business some thirty-three years ago at the age of seven when I pestered Jim Schoenherr, owner of Jim's Market, a corner grocery store, into letting me help fill sacks and perform other assorted jobs. By the time I was fifteen I had elevated myself to the meat department where, under the careful eye of Jim, I learned much about the art of meat cutting. Since I was working primarily for experience and the 'fun of it', not much attention was paid to whatever the Child Labor law might be.

My first restaurant job was in the Detroit suburb of Lathrup Village where, at the age of 15, I started as dishwasher and worked my way up to kitchen manager. From there I joined the Raleigh House in Southfield, Michigan and was in charge of the storeroom and equipment of what was at that time the largest indoor catering service in America.

In 1972 I answered an ad for Chuck Muer's Charley's Crab restaurant at Pine Lake as a management trainee, starting an eight year association which had me managing and trouble shooting Muer restaurants in the greater Detroit area, Ohio and Pennsylvania. At the age of twenty three, I assisted in the opening and, for two years, ran the 500 seat Grand Concourse restaurant in Pittsburgh's Station Square. By age twenty five I was Director of Restaurants of Detroit's Pontchartrain Hotel. I would be remiss if I did not give a special acknowledgment to the Muer Corporation and in fact to two special influences in my life. First, Chuck Muer. Tragically, Chuck and his wife Betty and another couple were lost at sea in a storm in March of 1993. Chuck always seemed to believe in me and his friendship meant a great deal to both Linda and me. I was proud to have been a member of his team and he is surely missed by a lot of others that he influenced. Second, my mentor, Jim Macdonald. Jim always gave me the opportunity to succeed or fail, whatever my talents

"In the beautiful north country of Leelanau Pennisula is an excellent restaurant, the Leelanau Country Inn. It starts with a pleasant greeting by the hostess and staff and leads to a great dinner and finishes with a fantastic dessert; our favorite, Brandied Peaches."
-Mr. & Mrs. Richard Wolanski

[Note: The recipe for Brandied Peaches does not appear in this book, as it is a well-guarded secret of the Inn.]

would produce. There are few I have learned more from. Thanks just does not seem to be enough, but thanks Jim, just the same.

The years of self-induced pressure, vacation-less work and incredibly long hours had taken their toll. I left the Muer Corporation June 3, 1980 and moved north. I was familiar with Northern Michigan. My twin sister, Jill, and I had spent most of our youth summering at Torch Lake, where our grandfather had been one of the region's early settlers. When a dear friend, Paul, introduced me to Leland, on the beautiful Leelanau peninsula, I knew I had found a home.

There, in June of 1980 at Leland's Riverside Inn, I met the lovely Linda Petersen. Linda was born and raised in Leland and I quickly realized that she was either related to, or at least knew, most everyone on the peninsula. Linda started young at the Blue Bird Restaurant in Leland and worked various positions, mainly performing as a waitress. Linda and I shared many of the same interests, and fifteen months later were married, with the reception held at the Riverside Inn, where we first met.

"Sandy & I have been regular 'guests' of the finest dining in Northern Michigan for all ten years the Leelanau Country Inn has blessed our area. Believe me we have tested the cuisine at every comparative restaurant in the north only to affirm that number one is right around the corner on M-22 in Leelanau County. My wife loves the excellent 'process' of eating at the Inn and I am crazy about the 'product' served on the platter. In fact the service and the food are the finest and we both thank John & Linda for a decade of customer happiness they have provided at the Leelanau Country Inn."
  -Mr. & Mrs. Don Miller

Within a couple of weeks after I arrived in Leland I became actively involved in consulting work with several restaurant operations and, shortly prior to the time Linda and I were married, I accepted the position of Food and Beverage Manager of the Milwaukee Hilton. The lure of Leelanau was too great, though. Eight months later we returned, and, for the next two years, I was Operations Manager and Food and Beverage Director of Traverse City's Park Place Hotel.

In 1984, we purchased the Leelanau Country Inn. It had been built 94 years earlier as the private home of the Fred Atkinson family. In 1900, major additions were made. It was christened the Traverse Lake Resort, and has housed travelers, under various ownerships, since then.

We opened our doors on the 20th of May and over the past ten years have welcomed some 500,000 guests. During that time the Inn has increased its seating from 100 to 150 by adding a side porch area. It has tripled the size of its kitchen operation and, in so doing, created what is thought to be the only temperature controlled preparation room in the area; every refrigerated product served is prepped under refrigeration. It does not hit the heat of the kitchen until it's time to be cooked.

I purchase all food and it is inspected on arrival by myself, or Lou or Matt, who have been with the Inn since its opening. The cooking staff is not only trained at the restaurant, it is also sent to Boston at regular intervals for courses in such areas as fish cutting, product handling and seafood marketing

All staff members are thoroughly trained for the positions they hold. The wait staff is provided with a documented training manual that reviews all areas relating to service and to the product. Ongoing training is given to be sure that nothing has been forgotten or overlooked. It is our strong belief that the only way to totally serve the guest is to insure that the staff has all of the necessary tools and product knowledge.

The Leelanau Country Inn menu, which is Northern Michigan's most extensive, is printed daily. All of its items are prepared by recipe to insure consistency from visit to visit. All products are prepped daily and cooked to order the night of service. While the Inn specializes in seafood and fresh fish from the ocean (provided by Connolly Seafood of Boston) and Michigan lakes (provided by Carlson's Fish Market of Traverse City), there are also a wide variety of meats and fresh homemade pasta with a generous array of exciting sauces. Our signature soup,

"A Candlelight dinner at a cozy Inn in the winter.
"The freshness of a country garden in the spring.
"Warm, friendly faces and aromas of delicious food being served.
"It's that special dining experience that keeps drawing us back to the Inn.
"Through the years you have been a part of many of our memorable occasions.
"Congratulations on the book and Happy Anniversary"
    -Mr. & Mrs. Warren Klinkner

Swiss Onion, has been featured in Gourmet and our wine list is comprised of the finest wines of Leelanau County, which is becoming a well respected and recognized wine producing region.

Diners can catch a glimpse of Little Traverse Lake across the road, marvel at the magnificent birch trees gracing the Inn's front yard, and take a stroll through the beautiful gardens, created by Linda and added to and nurtured by her over the years.

It has been a rewarding ten years for both of us, thanks to the many people who have worked with us in making the Leelanau Country Inn a favorite Northern Michigan dining spot and to the many guests who keep coming back and keep spreading the word.

To all of you we express our sincere gratitude.

-Linda Sisson

-John Sisson

The Wine List

"If a man deliberately abstains
from wine to such an extent
that he does serious harm
to his nature, he will not
be free from blame."

-Saint Thomas Aquinas

The wine list at the Leelanau Country Inn is nearly exclusively populated by the products of Leelanau Peninsula's four wineries. This is very much a European country inn style list, recognizing the local product as an integral part of one's daily life, with out-of-the-area wines and other foods served only as necessary for balance.

Locally produced wines offer us something special, in the same way that we enjoy tomatoes fresh from our backyard garden, or sweet corn picked and boiled immediately, or the juicy peach eaten under the tree on which it grew. Not only do these special foods taste good, but through them our immediate connection with the earth renews us. Those of us fortunate enough to live close to the land enjoy this connectedness and the urban or suburban dweller is drawn to places like Leelanau County by the desire for it. Fortunately, at places like the Country Inn, anyone has the opportunity to sit down and reestablish those natural connections in the company of family and friends.

But wine, unlike the fresh tomato, sweet corn, or peach, can travel through time as well as space. With wine, one can experience on a cold, bitter January day in 1995, the warmth, the joy, the life of the summer of 1991. Open a bottle of 1991 vintage, pour a glass, and smell the bouquet time has brought to the aromas of the grapes harvested years before, sip and savor the flavor of that season past, let it join in memory with the meal today. It is this ability to transcend time and place that has made wine such an intriguing part of our lives.

Sadly, all too often we are kept from this pleasureable

experience by our fear of doing something wrong. We have exhalted wine to a special place, surrounded it with mystery and ritual barely understood, and fear to intrude. This is unfortunate. For, though wine may be a mystery, its enjoyment, and its place at the table need not be. One surely does not need to know exactly how an airplane works, nor how to pilot it, in order to let an airline take you away to that longed for idyllic vacation spot. Neither do you need to know much about wine to let it grace your table.

About selecting and serving wine, there are no rules. Or, if you are a person who must have rules, then, there is only one rule - serve the wine you like, with the food you like. If guidance is desired, without the strictures of rulemaking, we can offer a few hints that will, we hope, increase your enjoyment of the meal and the wine. When matching wines with foods, consider the dominant flavor or aroma of the food, how intense it is; consider the flavors and aromas of the possible wine companions. If you are making a match that's intended to highlight the food, select a wine with complementary though less intense flavors and aromas - this wine will act like the second and third players in an orchestra section, deepening and filling in the sound of the first player, in this case the food. If you wish to highlight the wine, select an intensely flavored wine with flavors complementary to a lighter food, or (more difficult) a wine of intensity that contrasts with an intense food.

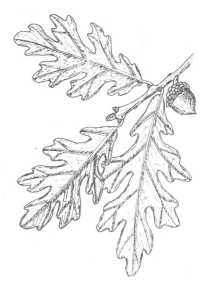

We have, in our own mind, divided the wines of Leelanau Peninsula into a few categories that make it easier to identify complementary and contrasting food and wine pairings. These categories are very simple, so simple in fact, that many wines don't really fit into the categories.

All sparkling wines are in a category of their own (from the Leelanau Peninsula, sparkling wines are almost always dry or very nearly so, with flavors and aromas hearkening to the classic French Champagnes). Honesty compels me to confess that I am currently the only producer of sparkling wines from the Leelanau Peninsula, so my description of them is not without prejudice.

When we encounter red wines, we've divided them into three categories - dry light red, dry medium red, and semi-dry red. There really aren't any heavy red wines produced in Leelanau (and this is one place the Country Inn balances the wine list with wines from elsewhere).

In the case of white wines from Leelanau Peninsula, the selection is much greater, and the range is larger. We've divided white wines into several categories - dry light white, dry medium white, dry heavy white, semi-dry light white, semi-dry medium white, and semi-dry heavy white. Since this categorization system is intended for offering suggestions with dinner entrees, we've not included any sweet wines (this is my personal preference, but, remember the rule - there are no rules - so if you wish, by all means enjoy a sweet wine, of any color and weight, with your meal).

Now what are dry, or semi-dry, wines? We mean by dry wines, those which have no perceptible sugary flavor. This does not mean that a dry wine might not have fruit flavors so intense that they bring to mind the memory of sweet, ripe fruit; but rather that they do not have a sugary character. Semi-dry wines, on the other hand, have some of this sugary character, though it is not dominant as would be the case with a sweet wine. Semi-dry wines live in both the dry and sweet worlds, partaking of a bit of both characters. My personal preference amongst semi-dry wines, with most foods, is for wines which smell of sweet fruits, taste initially of ripe, fresh fruit, and then, in the back of the mouth, display a pleasant crispness that refreshes the palate.

So, too, we have given three weights of wine: light, medium, and heavy. This has nothing to do with any scale measure, but is rather the sum of several parts of the perception of the wine. For me, the weight of the wine is what others call 'body' plus other factors like tannin, fruit intensity, even color. Light wines have minimal tannins (tannins produce the sensation of astringency, like the 'bite' of tea); generally lower levels of alcohol (alcohol contributes to the feel of the wine in the mouth, more alcohol making the wine feel 'fuller, rounder' and also 'hotter'); and generally the fruit flavors play a greater part in the totality of the wine's flavor, though they will themselves be lesser in intensity in a light wine than in a heavy wine. Heavy wines are at the other end of the taste spectrum, with much more tannic astringency, generally a greater weight of alcohol, and with other flavors (often those contributed by oak barrel aging) that underly or surround the fruit flavors inherent in the wine, bouying and making more massive the entire flavor structure. Obviously, medium weight wines strike some balance between the two poles, and represent the majority of all wines. Also, the medium weight wines are the most easily paired with entrees, as they can play second string to a spicy dish, or be the first string when playing with a delicately flavored entree.

Using the descriptors above, and this simple categorization system, should help you in communicating your desires when purchasing wine, either in a store or a restaurant. Any trained wine sales person can point out several candidates if asked, for example, for a dry, medium weight white wine. Later in this book, in the entree recipes, we offer specific wine suggestions, identified by these categories. This should help you find substitute wines, if you are unable to find a specific suggested wine (unfortunately, Leelanau Peninsula wines are, like fresh fish, not universally available, so substitutes are sometimes necessary). Generally, wine suggestions made later are intended to complement, rather than contrast with, the foods, and tend toward 'safe' matches - medium weight, semi-dry or dry wines. We've included two suggestions for each entree, with a specific example of a Leelanau Peninsula wine in each case.

And what of the producers of the wines on the list at the Country Inn? Today four wineries and over a dozen individual vineyards grace the Leelanau Peninsula. This Land of Delight is blessed with picturesque rolling hills, clear lakes and streams, clean air, and a charming diversity of seasons. Agriculture has been an important part of the life of the peninsula since modern settlement in the 1800's. Most recently, starting in the early 1970's, winegrape growing and wine making came to the Leelanau. More vines are being planted each year, and production of the area's dry red and white, semi-dry white and sparkling wines continues to increase.

Boskydel Vineyard, located south of the village of Lake Leelanau, on a hillside overlooking the lake, is the area's oldest winery. Bernie Rink pioneered winegrape growing in this area, first planting a small backyard vineyard in 1963. Further plantings followed, and a winery was established in 1976. Today Boskydel produces a range of dry and semi-dry, red, white and rosé table wines from several direct producer varieties grown in those vineyards. Boskydel is perhaps best known for dry and semi-dry reds and rosés from the deChaunac grape variety and dry and semi-dry whites from Vignoles and Seyval. Soleil Blanc is a unique dry white produced from a direct producer variety grown nowhere else.

Good Harbor Vineyards, located south of Leland with the winery overlooking Good Harbor Bay and with additional vineyards near Sugar Loaf Mountain, is the largest grower in the Peninsula. Bruce Simpson's Good Harbor vineyards, first planted in 1978, today produce a range of

dry and semi-dry, red, white and rosé table wines from
several vinifera and direct producer varieties, as well as a
particularly pleasant cherry wine. The winery is best
known for a series of excellent semi-dry white wines, such
as Trillium and Fishtown White; dry whites from
Vignoles, Chardonnay and Pinot Gris, and a semi-dry
white, Riesling.

Leelanau Wine Cellars, the second oldest winery in the
peninsula, is the largest producer. The winery is located at
Omena, with vineyards there and also southwest of
Suttons Bay. Again, the winery produces a range of wines,
primarily from direct producer varieties, with increasing
amounts of vinifera, that has included at times dessert
wines like ports or ice wines, in addition to red, white,
and rosé table wines, dry, semi-dry and sweet. The main-
stays of the winery are the semi-dry 'seasonal blends',
Winter White, Spring Splendor, and Summer Sunset; the
dry red and white Vis a Vis; and dry whites from Vignoles
and Chardonnay. The fruit wines of Leelanau Wine
Cellars are also notable.

L. Mawby Vineyards, the smallest producer, is located in
the hills south of Suttons Bay, with vineyards adjacent to
the winery. Our vineyards were established in 1973, and
additional plantings have been made subsequently, today
yielding a range of dry and semi-dry, red, white and rosé
table wines and sparkling wines, from both direct producer and vinifera varieties. We are perhaps best known as
a producer of methode champenoise sparkling wines, dry
whites from Vignoles and Pinot Gris, and semi-dry whites
like Sandpiper and PGW Pun.

In addition to the four wineries of the Leelanau Peninsula,
several individual growers have wine grape vineyards.
Many of these vineyards have been planted since 1990,
and are only just beginning to be productive. Most of
these growers sell their grapes to the local wineries,

supplying a portion of the grape needs of the winery, and some growers have ambitions to launch their own wineries. As the wines of these new vineyards become available, the wine list at the Leelanau Country Inn seems certain to grow, broadening the connection between the dinner table and the land, continuing to fulfill the Inn's promise of fine food and wine from the Land of Delight.

-Larry Mawby

COOKERY
FUNDAMENTALS

"A Titch in Thyme"
-Frank Sisson

There are many fundamental principles that underlie the instructions given in any cookbook. We've attempted in this section to detail the important assumptions we've made in writing *this* cookbook. These include details about preparation techniques, ingredient selection, cookery tools, and serving.

As you read through the recipes, you will note that three symbols are used to direct your attention to additional information.

♣ The Shamrock, found next to the recipe name in the Table of Contents and on the page with the recipe, means that some additional preparation time is required. This additional time may range from a few hours, in the case of dishes that must be well chilled before serving, to a day or more, in the case of marinated dishes or recipes that use sauces best made in advance in order that flavors may meld. In any case, the preparation instructions for the recipe will give you an idea of how much extra time is required.

Δ The Pyramid, found alongside an ingredient listing or in the preparation instructions, directs your attention to a Hint about the recipe, found after the preparation instructions. Hints are meant to help you with preparation techniques, or explain why a particular preparation method is used. If several Hints are included with a recipe, they are numbered, for example, Δ2.

◊ The Diamond, seen generally alongside an ingredient, directs you to a Variation for the recipe, found after the hints which follow the preparation instructions. Variations generally refer to substitute ingredients that may be used, though in some cases they may include additional ingredients or preparation steps. The Variations sometimes include changes in basic ingredients which, if used, re-make the recipe to yield a new dish. If several Variations are included with a recipe, they are numbered, for example, ◊3.

THE SETS The first rule of cookery is to take time to read the recipe before starting to make the dish, then assemble all required equipment and ingredients, chopping, dicing, slicing, etc, as required. This assemblage of equipment and ingredients is called The Set. Only after these preparations are made is The Set ready and the assembly of the dish to commence. Following this fundamental rule is of particular importance in these recipes, as many include as part of their ingredients the product of another recipe elsewhere in the book. Planning is essential to the preparation of virtually every entree recipe in this book. And with planning, preparation is simple.

FRESH FISH We feel that giving suggested substitutes for particular fresh fishes called for is particularly important, as availability of specific fishes will vary with the time of year and your proximity to sources of supply. In only a few cases are any but fresh fish called for - generally we do not recommend using frozen fish, and urge you to seek out a purveyor of the freshest, highest quality fish and seafood. At the Inn, only fresh (or out of season, fresh chilled) fish and seafood, available locally or flown in from Boston, is used. Commercial ocean fishing vessels are generally at sea for up to a week, catching fish each day. Our fresh fish is Pure Fresh™ fish that is caught on the last day of the fishing trip (called 'top of the trip'), processed and flown to us so that it arrives at the Inn only one day out of the water. We buy Georges Banks fish, caught in the cold, clear Atlantic waters off the continental shelf some 150 miles from shore. Fresh chilled fish are these Pure Fresh™ fish, chilled to minus 40 degrees one day out of water, then held at minus 20 degrees until use, truly pure and fresh. We use these fresh chilled fish only when fresh is seasonally unavailable.

Frozen Fish If you must use frozen fish, a useful technique to help restore moisture and therefore texture to the prepared dish is to marinate the thawed fillet or steak in milk. Place fillet or steak in a shallow, sealable container, cover with fresh milk, seal and refrigerate for 24 hours. Before cooking, drain and discard milk, but do not pat fish dry, allowing a bit of moisture to remain.

We cannot emphasize too strongly the importance in cookery of quality ingredients. Time spent searching out sources of fresh fish, poultry and other quality meats is well spent, and rewarded at the table. Many dishes in this book call for fresh vegetables, and we recommend that those dishes be prepared seasonally as the required vegetables are available in your locality, either from your own garden or a local market garden or farmer's market. Frozen ingredients are called for where they will not compromise quality, or where there is generally no fresh ingredient available.

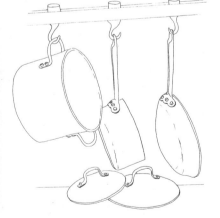

Cookware Three basic pans are used on top of the stove: the sauté pan, the sauce pan, and the soup pot. Generally, a skillet or frying pan is identical to a sauté pan. Where crepes are made, a crepe pan is preferred, but skillful use of a small sauté pan will suffice. In some cases, cast iron is called for - especially in blackening fish or meat - and any substitution would be ill advised. Sauce pans come in many sizes, and differ from soup pots in the matter of handles. Both sauce pans and soup pots are cylindrical vessels with removable lids. Sauce pans have a single long handle jutting out of one side, while soup pots have a pair of short handles attached to opposite side of the pot. At the Inn, we prefer pots and pans that round from the bottom to the sides, rather than those that have square transitions, as the rounded style is easier to clean thoroughly. Casseroles & baking dishes are oven-proof dishes used to bake many dishes, and are used either covered or uncovered, as the recipe directs. Sheet pans are used for baking cookies and other desserts, some fish fillets, etc. They're flat, with low or no sides, and allow air circulated by a convection oven to move freely around the food being baked.

HERBS & SPICES The assumption in all recipes in this book is that dried herbs and spices are used, as most home kitchens will not have ready access to fresh at all times of the year. Occasionally, fresh herbs or spices are used, and are so noted. If you wish to use fresh herbs or spices where we have assumed that dried will be used, it may be necessary to make adjustments to the quantity used, to avoid varying the intensity of spicing.

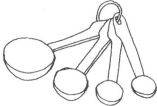

TITCH Salt and pepper are generally used to taste. In many recipes, specific quantities will be called for and sometimes the amount needed is smaller than ⅛ tsp (the smallest standard measure). In those cases, we have called for a titch, which is our measure for a quantity less than ⅛ tsp, but more than nothing. A titch is smaller than a pinch.

PAPRIKA Several types of paprika are available, the most common being either Hungarian or Spanish. In these recipes, the use of Spanish paprika is assumed.

PARSLEY When fresh parsley is used, carefully wash, dry and finely chop, unless the recipe specifically calls for sprigs of parsley, in which case, carefully wash and dry but do not chop. It is particularly important that fresh parsley be carefully dried when making breadings and stuffings as excess moisture will upset the recipe.

GARLIC Many of these recipes call for garlic puree, which is a very convenient form of fresh garlic, and used extensively at the Inn. If you wish, you can substitute finely minced fresh garlic cloves.

ONIONS When dicing onions, always chop the onions by hand with a sharp knife, rather than using a food processor. Processing onions draws moisture out of the onion: this moisture will make breadings too moist, and will spread onion flavor excessively in dishes like rice pilaf.

EGGS In all recipes, large eggs are assumed. If you wish to use medium size eggs in recipes calling for three or more eggs, increase the number of eggs used.

FLOUR Whenever flour is called for, all-purpose is the type used. Many recipes call for flour that will be used to dredge some ingredients. The amount of flour called for is the quantity needed to work with in dredging - but is not meant to be entirely used up in the process. Some dredging flour will be left over, and if clean and dry may be saved for later use. If in doubt, discard remaining dredging flour.

ENCRUTE EnCrutes are anything baked in a pastry shell, generally poultry, meat, or fish, though vegetable enCrutes are possible. Beef Wellington is perhaps the most well known enCrute dish.

PASTA At the Inn we use fresh pasta prepared in our kitchens. However, for these recipes, we have not made the assumption that you will be preparing fresh pasta. If you can make your own, by all means do so. If fresh pasta is available from a local grocery or specialty food store, use that. If you use dried pasta, follow preparation instructions on the package carefully, and *do not overcook.*

IQF This stands for Individually Quick Frozen, and refers to a method of freezing fruit, shrimp and other foods. Many of the recipes that call for frozen fruit call for this type. It should be available in most grocery store freezer sections. We use IQF fruit because the individual pieces (in the case of cherries or raspberries, for example, individual fruits) are frozen separately, allowing you to remove from the freezer and use only what you need without thawing any excess. Also, the fruit does not have added sugar, and, generally, only the most attractive and best flavored fruit is frozen in this manner.

LEMON Lemon crowns are always served with fish and seafood entrees at the Inn. We've not included them in any list of ingredients unless they are actually used in preparation, but recommend the service of fresh lemon with fish and seafood entrees, particularly at a formal dinner party.

WOOKIES At the Inn, Cheese Wookies (Pg 214) are served with every salad. We've included them here in the dessert section, as they are nice little cookies to serve as hor d'oevures with sparkling wine, or with fresh fruit for dessert, as well as to complement green salads.

MARINADES Never re-use a marinade. In some cases, the marinade will have given up all flavor and be too weak to be used again. At other times the marinade will have picked up flavors from the marinated item, and would transfer those flavors to the next item. In all cases, once the marinade has done its job, discard it.

SCROD VS SCHROD Debate rages in the culinary community about the proper spelling of this word. We've chosen to use Schrod, as it is John's favored spelling, and the one used by Steve Connolly Seafood. Note also that we've chosen to capitalize all fish names - making them stand out from surrounding text and making them easier to read, we think.

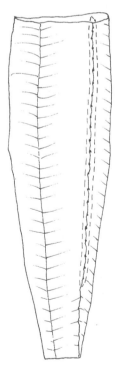

STEAKS & FILLETS Fresh fish is sold in three principal ways: in the round, as steaks, or as fillets. In the round is the whole fish, entrails removed, usually with the head and tail in place. A fish steak is a cut, usually of a large-sized fish that has had the entrails removed. The steak is a cross section of the fish with back and rib bones removed. A fillet, on the other hand, is a cut that runs lengthwise from gills to tail on one side of the fish, and also does not include the back or rib bones, though in some cases pin bones are still in fillets when you purchase them. In the case of large fish, fillets are taken from three areas along the length of the fish, the head, middle, and tail. Unless otherwise called for, the best fillets are from the tail, as they are likely to have the fewest bones.

PIN BONES It is sometimes necessary to remove the pin bones from fillets. Here's how. Place fillet skin side down on a cutting board, and run your finger along the top side of the thickest part of the fillet. This is where the pin bones, if still in the fillet, are located. You can feel the ends of the bones as you run your hand along this thick section of the fillet. To remove the bones, you will make a V shaped cut, along the length of the fillet, centered on this line of bones. With a sharp knife, starting at the head end of the fillet about ⅛ inch to the left of the pin bone line, cut about ¾ of the way through the fillet, angling right under the pin bones, and draw the knife down along the pin bone line to the tail end of the fillet. Make another cut, parallel to the first, beginning again at the head end of the fillet, this time ⅛ inch to the right of the pin bone line and angling left under the bones. The bottom of this cut should meet the bottom of the first cut. As you draw the knife down the line of bones to the tail, you will produce a V shaped cut that contains all the pin bones. This section of fish is then removed and discarded. The fillet is now de-boned and ready for further preparation.

BREADINGS, STUFFINGS, SAUCES & DRESSINGS

"People who like this sort
of thing will find this the
sort of thing they like."
-Abraham Lincoln

HERBAL BREADING

YIELD   3 CUPS

Cooks Notes

INGREDIENTS

2¾ Cups	Dried Bread Crumbs Δ
¼ Lb	Romano Cheese - grated
1 Tbl	Thyme Leaf
1 Tbl	Basil Leaf
1 Tbl	Whole Oregano
1 Tbl	Garlic Puree
2 Tbls	Fresh Parsley - chopped

PREPARATION
Thoroughly mix all ingredients.

HINTS
May be stored under refrigeration for 1 - 2 months.
Δ This breading requires very fine bread crumbs. If
'Japanese style', i.e. coarse crumbs, are available, process
for 1 or 2 minutes in a food processor to reduce the size of
the crumb.

USES
Useful breading for shrimp, chicken, steaks and chops; for
either baking or frying.

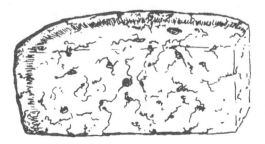

ALMONDINE BREADING

YIELD   2¼ CUPS

INGREDIENTS   *Cooks Notes*

2 Cups	Dried Bread Crumbs Δ
1	Lemon - zest only, finely grated
½ Cup	Almonds - sliced

PREPARATION
Thoroughly mix all ingredients.

HINTS
May be stored under refrigeration for 1 -2 months.
Δ This breading requires very fine bread crumbs. If
'Japanese style', i.e. coarse crumbs, are available, process
for 1 or 2 minutes in a food processor to reduce the size of
the crumb.

USES
This breading is used with any pan-fried or oven-baked
fish.

APPLE BREAD STUFFING

YIELD   4 CUPS

Cooks Notes

INGREDIENTS

4 Cups	Dried Bread Cubes (¼") Δ ◊
4 Cups	Water
4 tsp	Wyler's Chicken Bouillon
1 Cup	Onions - diced
1 Cup	Celery - diced
2 Cups	Apples - sliced
1 Tbl	Cinnamon - ground
1 Tbl	Poultry Seasoning

PREPARATION

In a deep sauce pan or soup pot, mix water and chicken bouillon; then add onions, celery, apples, cinnamon and poultry seasoning, and bring to a boil. Add bread cubes, stir thoroughly, cool and refrigerate until ready to use.

HINTS

This stuffing will keep under refrigeration for up to two weeks, or can be frozen and held for up to six months. When using frozen stuffing, allow to thaw, and check moisture content - a small addition of water may be necessary.

Δ Vary the amount of bread used to increase or decrease the moistness of the stuffing.

VARIATIONS

◊ Herbed, rye, or whole wheat bread may be used to vary the flavor.

The addition of dried tart cherries gives this stuffing another dimension.

USES

This stuffing is used for poultry or pork, including chops, crown roasts, and rolled roasts.

CRAB MEAT STUFFING

YIELD   4 CUPS

INGREDIENTS

Cooks Notes

2 Cups	Crab Meat Δ1 ◊1
½ Cup	Drawn Butter Δ2
½ Cup	Onions - finely chopped
¾ Cup	Bread Crumbs ◊2
1½ Cup	White Cream Sauce (pg 51)

PREPARATION

In a sauté pan, heat butter, add onions and sauté until tender. Set aside to cool Δ3. Add cool cream sauce, cool onions, crab meat and bread crumbs and mix well. Refrigerate and allow to set up, approximately one hour.

HINTS

May be stored, well sealed, under refrigeration for 7 - 10 days; or frozen for 1 - 2 months.

Δ1 Be careful to remove any cartilage from the crab meat you buy.

Δ2 To make drawn butter, melt butter, allow solids to settle, and carefully pour off liquid. This liquid is drawn butter, and may be cooled and stored for later use. Plan to lose 25 - 35 percent of the beginning volume.

Δ3 It is very important that hot and cold items are not mixed together as this can cause the stuffing to sour.

VARIATIONS

◊1 We use Cape Cod Jonah Stone Crab - it is a sweet crab and the flakes make an excellent stuffing. King Crab, Blue Crab or another favorite of yours may be used as well. Avoid imitation crab!

◊2 We use plain bread crumbs in this stuffing. Feel free to use herbal or seasoned crumbs if you prefer. Keep in mind, however, that the stuffing should not have an overpowering flavor.

USES

This stuffing is used in several freshwater and ocean fishes, shellfish, and shrimp; also stuffed mushroom caps.

FLORENTINE STUFFING

YIELD 3½ CUPS

Cooks Notes

INGREDIENTS

2 Lb	Frozen Spinach - chopped
3½ Tbls	Canola Oil
4½ Tbls	Butter
6 slices	Bacon - diced
¾ Cup	Onions - finely chopped
¾ Cup	Dry White Table Wine ◊
1 Tbl	Garlic Puree

PREPARATION

Squeeze spinach dry Δ. Chop and set aside. In a sauté pan heat oil and butter over medium heat. Add bacon, cooking until crispy and well rendered. Add onions and sauté a couple of minutes. Add spinach, garlic and wine and simmer for 3 minutes. Cool and refrigerate for at least one hour before use.

HINTS

May be stored, well sealed, under refrigeration for 7 - 10 days; or frozen for 1 - 2 months.
Δ It is important that the spinach be as dry as possible, as excessive moisture results in stuffing that will not hold together. To dry spinach, place the spinach in the center of a kitchen towel, bring up the sides and twist the cloth to squeeze out excess moisture.

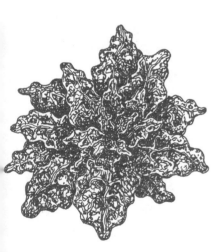

VARIATIONS

◊ The white wine may be replaced with sherry; or to make a heartier florentine, with a dry red wine.

USES

This stuffing is used in several freshwater and ocean fishes, shellfish, and shrimp; also poultry and mushrooms.

PUNGENT FRUIT SAUCE

YIELD   1¼ CUPS

INGREDIENTS   *Cooks Notes*

15.5 oz Jar	Orange Marmalade ◊
3 Tbls	Horseradish
1 Tbl	Fresh Lemon Juice
1 tsp	Dry Mustard
1 tsp	Ginger - ground
⅛ tsp	Tabasco Sauce

PREPARATION

Combine all ingredients in a blender and blend for 15 - 20 seconds.
Serve at room temperature or chilled.

HINTS

May be stored under refrigeration for up to 3 weeks. We do not recommend freezing this sauce.

VARIATIONS

◊ We recommend Smuckers Low Sugar Orange Marmalade Spread

USES

This sauce is a fine accompaniment to poultry entrees, or pork tenderloin. Also used atop cream cheese as a cracker spread.

RASPBERRY SAUCE

YIELD   2¼ CUPS

Cooks Notes

INGREDIENTS

12 oz Pkg	IQF Frozen Raspberries
2 Cups	Water ◊
½ Cup	Brown Sugar
2 Tbls	Honey
Thickening	
2 Tbls	Corn Starch
¼ Cup	Cold Water

PREPARATION

In a sauce pan, bring water, raspberries, brown sugar and honey to a rapid boil. Make thickening in a separate container by adding corn starch and rapidly stirring in cold water, mixing completely Δ. Then slowly add thickening to the boiling raspberry mixture. When sauce returns to a boil, remove from heat.

HINTS

May be stored under refrigeration for up to 30 days.
Δ To improve mixing, add cold water to the corn starch, rather than corn starch to the water.

VARIATIONS

◊ Replacing some of the water with a flavored brandy will create a different and exciting sauce.

USES

This sauce enhances any poultry, pork or veal dish.

DRIED CHERRY GLAZE

YIELD   1½ CUPS

INGREDIENTS

Cooks Notes

1 Cup	Water
1 tsp	Wyler's Beef Bouillon
½ Cup	Dried Tart Cherries
1 Tbl	Honey
1 Tbl	Brown Sugar
1 Tbl	Dry Sherry Wine ◊

Thickening
1 Tbl	Corn Starch
2 Tbls	Cold Water

PREPARATION

In a sauce pan, mix water and bouillon. Add honey, brown sugar and sherry and bring to a boil. Make thickening in a separate container by adding corn starch and rapidly stirring in cold water, mixing completely. Δ Then slowly add to boiling mixture and stir till the glaze thickens. Remove from heat and stir in dried cherries.

HINTS

Δ To improve mixing, add cold water to the corn starch, rather than corn starch to the water.
This glaze may be stored for up to 30 days under refrigeration.

VARIATIONS

◊ Sherry may be replaced with flavored brandy.

USES

Use with poultry, veal, ham and other pork entrees.

LEMON BUTTER SAUCE

YIELD   1½ CUPS

Cooks Notes

INGREDIENTS

1 Cup	Fresh Lemon Juice
1 Lb	Butter - cubed

PREPARATION
Bring lemon juice to a boil and remove from heat. Place butter, cut into small pieces, into the lemon juice a piece at a time and stir vigorously Δ until melted.

HINTS
May be stored under refrigeration for up to one month or frozen for at least six months. However, will not work by itself as a sauce after storage, see Uses.
Δ For a smoother and thicker sauce, use a high speed hand held mixer: you cannot over mix this sauce.

VARIATIONS
Add favorite seasonings to create a personal sauce: fresh basil for a lemon basil butter, capers for a great piccata sauce, pecan pieces for a lemon pecan butter sauce.

USES
As a freshly prepared sauce, use with vegetables, poultry and fish. After refrigerated or frozen storage, may be used as the base for another batch of this sauce, by addition of more fresh lemon juice and butter, or may be used as is to replace butter in several recipes, wherever you would like a bit of lemon flavor.

Garlic Butter Sauce

Yield   2½ Cups

Ingredients

Cooks Notes

1 Lb	Butter - softened
⅛ tsp	White Pepper - ground
1 Tbl	Garlic Puree
2 tsp	Anchovy Paste
2 Tbls	Fresh Parsley - chopped
2 Tbls	Green Pepper - finely chopped
2 Tbls	Red Pepper - finely chopped
¼ Cup	Dry White Wine ◊

Preparation

Soften butter by letting it sit out at room temperature for at least 2 hours. In a power mixing bowl add all ingredients except wine, and mix. Slowly add the wine and mix until the wine has been completely absorbed Δ by the butter and the sauce peaks.

Hints

May be frozen for storage, for up to six months, or refrigerated for up to one month.
Δ It is important that the wine be well mixed to prevent later separation.

Variations

◊ For use with red meats, replace the dry white wine with a dry red wine.

Uses

May be used for sautéing nearly anything, as a spread on French or Italian loaves, or as a base sauce for escargot.

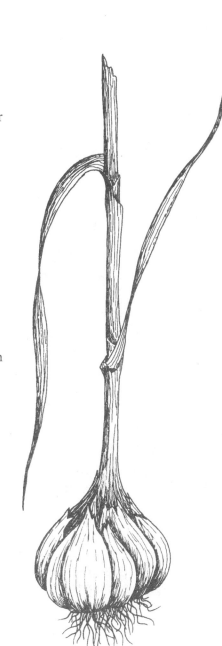

MUSTARD BUTTER

YIELD   ½ CUP

Cooks Notes

INGREDIENTS

6 Tbls	Butter - softened
3 Tbls	Lemon Juice
4 tsp	Country Dijon Mustard ◊
¾ tsp	Salt
½ tsp	Paprika

PREPARATION
Soften butter by allowing to sit at room temperature for at least 2 hours. In a mixing bowl, combine the butter, lemon juice, mustard, salt and paprika, mixing all ingredients together by hand.

HINTS
May be stored under refrigeration for up to one month, or frozen for up to six months.

VARIATIONS
◊ For a little less 'bite', plain Dijon may be substituted for the country style Dijon.

USES
A great complement to any full flavored fish, or as a sandwich spread with hot ham sandwiches, hamburgers, etc.

PECAN BUTTER SAUCE

YIELD   1 CUP

INGREDIENTS   *Cooks Notes*

¼ Lb   Butter - softened
¾ Cup   Pecan Pieces
¾ Tbl   Lemon Juice
1 tsp   Tabasco Sauce ◊
½ tsp   Garlic Puree

PREPARATION
Soften butter by allowing to sit at room temperature for at
least 2 hours. In a mixing bowl, combine butter, pecan
pieces, lemon juice, Tabasco sauce, garlic puree, mixing all
ingredients together by hand. With your hands, form the
mixture into a cylindrical log about one inch in diameter,
roll up in parchment paper, twist the ends of the paper
tight and store in the refrigerator Δ.

HINTS
May be stored under refrigeration for up to one month.
Δ For longer term storage, rather than rolling the sauce in
a piece of parchment paper, divide evenly into an ice cube
tray, seal, and freeze; may be stored frozen for up to six
months.

VARIATIONS
◊ Vary the amount of Tabasco sauce used to change the
intensity of flavor. Without the Tabasco sauce the pecan
butter is a milder, yet flavorful, topping useful for many
fish and chicken entrees.

USES
Cut into ¼ inch thick portions and place on top of
blackened entrees (meat, fish, or poultry) after cooking,
just before serving.

MUSTARD SAUCE

YIELD   3½ CUPS

Cooks Notes

INGREDIENTS

1 Cup	Water
1 tsp	Wyler's Beef Bouillon
2 Tbls	Margarine
4 Tbls	Onions - diced
¼ Cup	Carrots - shredded
2 Tbls	Flour
2 Cups	Tomatoes - diced
2 Tbls	Smoked Ham - finely diced
¼ Cup	Prepared Mustard
1	Bay Leaf
⅛ tsp	Thyme Leaf

PREPARATION

In a mixing bowl, mix water with bouillon and set aside.
In a sauce pan, melt margarine, add onions and carrots
and sauté until tender. Add flour, mix well and cook for 5
minutes on low heat. Add bouillon and water mixture and
diced tomatoes, mixing well. Add remaining ingredients
and simmer for 20 minutes. Stir constantly to reduce
sticking.

HINTS

May be stored under refrigeration for up to two weeks.

USES

Best when used with pork and veal entrees.

TERIYAKI SAUCE

YIELD   2 CUPS

INGREDIENTS   *Cooks Notes*

1 Cup	Soy Sauce
½ Cup	Red Wine Vinegar
½ Cup	Water
½ tsp	Wyler's Chicken Bouillon
1 Tbl	Honey
1 Tbl	Sugar
1 Tbl	Garlic Puree
2 Tbls	Prepared Mustard
⅛ tsp	Salt
⅛ tsp	White Pepper - ground

PREPARATION

Mix all ingredients together and bring to a boil. Simmer for 30 minutes, allow to cool before use.

HINTS

May be stored for 2 -3 months under refrigeration.

USES

Use in stir fried vegetables; also makes a great marinade for poultry, veal, pork, or beef.

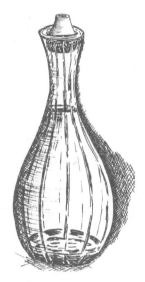

CAJUN SPICE

YIELD   2 CUPS

INGREDIENTS

½ Cup	Paprika
⅓ Cup	White Pepper - ground
⅓ Cup	Black Pepper - coarse ground
⅓ Cup	Cayenne Pepper
⅓ Cup	Thyme Leaf
¼ Cup	Whole Oregano
2 Tbls	Basil Leaf

PREPARATION
Carefully mix ingredients together Δ.

HINTS
Store sealed under refrigeration, virtually forever.
Δ Be careful not to breathe deeply while mixing. This is a very potent spice mixture.

USES
Used to blacken nearly anything - fish, seafood, poultry, meat. Traditional blackening is a searing on high heat, usually in an iron skillet. This mixture may be used to 'blacken' baked dishes by sprinkling on top prior to baking.

WHITE CREAM SAUCE

YIELD   2 CUPS

INGREDIENTS   *Cooks Notes*

2 Tbls   Canola Oil
3 Tbls   Flour
2 Cups   Milk

PREPARATION

In a sauce pan, heat oil. Add flour, stirring continuously.
Cook for about 5 minutes, nearly boiling the roux,
carefully stirring to prevent scorching. At the same time
bring milk to a scald. Mix the hot milk and the roux
together, stirring vigorously. ◊

HINTS

May be stored, sealed, under refrigeration for up to seven
days, if milk used in sauce has an expiration date at least
that far in the future.
◊ Have milk and roux very hot prior to mixing. This will
bring the sauce to a smooth, medium thick consistency
quickly, with less stirring.

VARIATIONS

Wine, flavored brandy or liqueur, or herbs such as fresh
basil, fresh dill or fresh rosemary may be added to create a
variety of flavored cream sauces.

USES

This sauce is a basic component of some stuffings and
cream sauced dishes.

Sweet Tartar Sauce

Yield   1¼ Cups

Cooks Notes

Ingredients

1 Cup	Mayonnaise
2 Tbls	Onions - chopped
1 Tbl	Capers - chopped
½ Tbl	Fresh Parsley - chopped
2 Tbls	Sweet Relish
½ Tbl	Horseradish
2 tsp	Chives

Preparation
Chop onions, capers and parsley. Add to mayonnaise, sweet relish, horseradish and chives, mixing all ingredients well.

Hints
May be stored, sealed, under refrigeration for up to 30 days.

Uses
A useful accent to many fish dishes; and a flavorful base for shrimp salad.

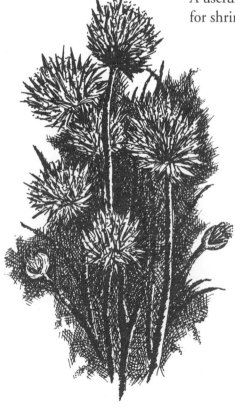

DILLED TARTAR SAUCE

YIELD   1¾ CUPS

INGREDIENTS   *Cooks Notes*

1 Cup	Mayonnaise
½ Cup	Dill Relish
3 Tbls	Onions - chopped
1 Tbl	Fresh Parsley - chopped

PREPARATION
Chop onions and parsley, add to mayonnaise and dill
relish, mixing all ingredients together well.

HINTS
May be stored, sealed, under refrigeration for up to 30
days.

USES
A useful accent to many fish dishes

BEARNAISE SAUCE

YIELD   1½ CUPS

Cooks Notes

INGREDIENTS

1 Tbl	Whole Black Pepper - crushed
¼ Cup	Tarragon Vinegar
1 Cup	Drawn Butter Δ1
4	Egg Yolks
½ tsp	Tarragon Leaf
1 Tbl	Fresh Lemon Juice
⅛ tsp	Salt
Titch	Cayenne Pepper ◊

PREPARATION

Crush peppercorns with a rolling pin. In a sauce pan, combine crushed pepper with vinegar and cook until the volume has been reduced by half. Remove from heat and strain into a blender. With blender at a medium setting add warmed drawn butter very, very slowly. (The drawn butter should be warmed to prevent the sauce from breaking.) Add egg yolks, one at a time. Add lemon juice and a titch of cayenne pepper. Add tarragon and salt. Remove and place in a stainless steel bowl at room temperature. Δ2 Use immediately, do not attempt to store.

HINTS

Δ1 To make drawn butter, melt butter, allow solids to settle, and carefully pour off liquid. This liquid is drawn butter, and may be cooled and stored for later use. Plan to lose 25 - 35 percent of the beginning volume.

Δ2 If the sauce breaks at this point, add an ice cube to the mixture and stir vigorously. The sauce should return to the proper consistency.

VARIATIONS

◊ Cayenne pepper may be replaced with 4 drops of Tabasco sauce.

USES

Use with flavorful fish and seafood or beef encrutes.

Hollandaise Sauce

YIELD 1½ CUPS

INGREDIENTS

Cooks Notes

1 Lb	Butter
8	Whole Eggs
¼ Cup	Fresh Lemon Juice
	Salt & Pepper to Taste

PREPARATION

In a sauce pan, melt the butter and set aside. In a separate stainless pan, beat eggs over medium heat until medium thick. Slowly add melted butter to beaten eggs. If the mixture becomes too thick, add a small amount of lemon juice. When all the butter has been added and the sauce is a smooth consistency, add the remaining lemon juice. Salt and pepper to taste. Place the finished sauce in a clean stainless pan. Δ Use immediately, do not attempt to store.

HINTS

Δ If the sauce breaks at this point, add an ice cube to the mixture and stir vigorously. The sauce should return to the proper consistency.

USES

Use with fish, seafood, or vegetables. This is the traditional sauce for Eggs Benedict and Oscar dishes.

BARBECUE SAUCE ♣

YIELD   1½ CUPS

Cooks Notes

INGREDIENTS

1 Cup	Ketchup
1 Cup	Chili Sauce
2 Tbls	Brown Sugar
2 Tbls	Apple Cider Vinegar
2 tsp	Dry Mustard
2 Tbls	Water
¼ tsp	Black Pepper - ground
¼ tsp	Thyme Leaf
2 Tbls	Honey
4 Drops	Tabasco Sauce

PREPARATION
Mix all ingredients together well.

HINTS
Make one day before use if possible.
May be stored under refrigeration for 1 -2 months.

USES
For barbecuing fish, poultry, pork, beef.

MARINARA SAUCE ♣

YIELD   6 CUPS

INGREDIENTS   *Cooks Notes*

1 tsp	Canola Oil
1¼ Cups	Onion - finely chopped
½ Cup	Green Pepper - finely chopped
1 Tbl	Whole Oregano
½ tsp	Thyme Leaf
3 Tbls	Garlic Puree
3 Tbls	Fresh Parsley - chopped
1 Tbl	Wyler's Chicken Bouillon
1	Bay Leaf
2 Cups	Diced Tomatoes
2 Cups	Tomato Puree
1 tsp	Anchovy Paste
½ tsp	White Pepper - ground
2 tsp	Sugar
2 Cups	Water

PREPARATION

In a soup pot, heat oil and sauté onions, peppers, oregano, thyme, garlic, chicken bouillon and bay leaf until onions and peppers become limp. Add the remaining ingredients and simmer uncovered for 45 minutes, stirring occassionally.

HINTS

May be stored, sealed, under refrigeration for up to one month.
Marinara sauce is best when made the day before use; however, this sauce may be used immediately after cooking.

VARIATIONS

Add shrimp, scallops, or crab meat to make a seafood sauce.

USES

Use as a sauce over pasta, or to compliment grilled fish.

GREEK DRESSING ♣

YIELD   3 CUPS

Cooks Notes

INGREDIENTS

2 Cups	Canola Oil
¾ Cup	Apple Cider Vinegar
½ Tbl	Sugar
½ Tbl	Salt
¼ tsp	Basil Leaf
⅛ tsp	White Pepper - ground
½ Tbl	Whole Oregano
¾ Tbl	Garlic Puree

PREPARATION

Mix all ingredients together well.

HINTS

May be stored, sealed, under refrigeration for up to one month.

It is always best to make dressings at least a day ahead of use, to allow the flavors to marry.

USES

In addition to use as a lettuce or pasta salad dressing, this makes a great meat and poultry marinade.

CAESAR DRESSING ♣

YIELD   2 CUPS

INGREDIENTS   *Cooks Notes*

1 Tbl	Fresh Lemon Juice
4 Tbls	Country Dijon Mustard
1 Tbl	Garlic Puree
4	Egg Yolks
4 Tbls	Anchovy Paste
2 tsp	Worcestershire Sauce
1¼ Cup	Olive Oil

PREPARATION
In a blender, place all ingredients except olive oil and
blend on high speed for one minute. Then add the olive
oil, slowly, until blended well.

HINTS
May be stored, sealed, under refrigeration for up to one
month.
It is always best to make dressings at least a day ahead of
use, to allow the flavors to marry.

USES
A classic caesar salad dressing that is easy to make.

RASPBERRY VINIAGRETTE DRESSING

YIELD   4½ CUPS

INGREDIENTS

1 Cup	Raspberry Vinegar Δ
2 Cups	Canola Oil
1 Cup	Maple Syrup
¼ Cup	Country Dijon Mustard
¼ Cup	Tarragon Leaf
½ tsp	Salt

PREPARATION
Mix all ingredients together well.

HINTS
May be stored, sealed, under refrigeration for up to one month.
It is always best to make dressings at least a day ahead of use, to allow the flavors to marry.
Δ Raspberry Vinegar is available in most food specialty shops. However, should you wish to make your own, combine 1 Cup white vinegar and 1 Cup red wine vinegar and add ½ Cup fresh or frozen raspberries. Allow to stand for 36 hours, then strain out the raspberries.

USES
Use as a salad dressing, or as a fine fish, poultry, or meat marinade.

FRENCH DRESSING ♣

YIELD   5 CUPS

INGREDIENTS

Cooks Notes

1½ Cup	Sugar
15 oz Can	Condensed Tomato Soup
1⅛ Cup	Cider Vinegar
3½ tsp	Salt
3½ tsp	Black Pepper - ground
3½ tsp	Prepared Mustard
3½ tsp	Worcestershire Sauce
½ tsp	Garlic Puree
1¼ Cups	Canola Oil
¼	Onion

PREPARATION
In a mixing bowl, mix all ingredients, except the oil and onion, together well. Then add oil slowly while whipping, until dressing is well blended. Take one quartered peeled onion, separate the layers of the onion and add onion sections to dressing.

HINTS
May be stored, sealed, under refrigeration for up to one month.
It is always best to make dressings at least a day ahead of use, to allow the flavors to marry.

USES
In addition to it's primary use as a salad dressing, this also makes an excellent vegetable marinade.

ITALIAN DRESSING ♣

YIELD   3½ CUPS

Cooks Notes

INGREDIENTS

2 Cups	Canola Oil
1⅓ Cups	Red Wine Vinegar
1 tsp	Sugar
1 tsp	Salt
1 tsp	Basil Leaf
1 tsp	Fresh Parsley - chopped
1 tsp	Whole Oregano

PREPARATION
Mix all ingredients together well.

HINTS
May be stored, sealed, under refrigeration for up to one month.
It is always best to make dressings at least a day ahead of use, to allow the flavors to marry.

USES
Use as a lettuce or pasta salad dressing, to make an Italian style cole slaw, or to marinate poultry, meat or vegetables.

BLUE CHEESE DRESSING

YIELD 3 CUPS

INGREDIENTS   *Cooks Notes*

2 Cups	Mayonnaise
½ Cup	Blue Cheese - crumbled
1 Tbl	Buttermilk
2 Tbls	Beer ◊
2 Tbls	Romano Cheese - grated
2 Tbls	Sour Cream
¼ Cup	White Vinegar

PREPARATION
In a large mixing bowl, mix all ingredients together well.

HINTS
May be stored, sealed, under refrigeration for up to one month.
The harder you mix, the more broken the blue cheese becomes. If you prefer a large chuck style dressing, mix all the ingredients except the blue cheese together well first, then add the blue cheese and mix lightly.

VARIATIONS
◊ Beers of different flavors will affect the flavor of this dressing. Experiment to find your favorite.

USES
Commonly used as a garnish, with celery, for hot chicken wings in addition to use as a salad dressing.

Thousand Island Dressing

Yield   3 Cups

Cooks Notes

Ingredients

2 Cups	Mayonnaise
9 Tbls	Chili Sauce
2 Tbls	Dill Weed
2 Tbls	Chives
2 Tbls	Fresh Parsley - chopped
2 Tbls	Dill Pickle Relish
2 Tbls	Red Peppers - finely diced

Preparation
Mix all the ingredients together well.

Hints
May be stored, sealed, under refrigeration for up to one month.

Variations
If you prefer a sweeter Thousand Island, you may replace the dill pickle relish with a sweet pickle relish.

Uses
Traditional sauce for Reuben sandwiches, used also to add flair to a hamburger, as well as a useful salad dressing.

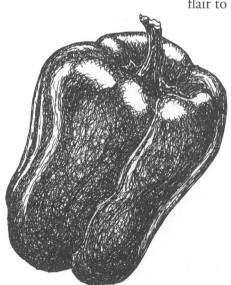

POPPY SEED DRESSING

YIELD   3 CUPS

INGREDIENTS   *Cooks Notes*

2¼ Cup   Sour Cream
4 Tbls   Butter - melted
½ Cup   Onions - diced
⅛ Cup   White Vinegar
¼ Cup   Sugar
1 Tbl   Poppy Seeds

PREPARATION
Mix all ingredients together and chill.

HINTS
May be stored, sealed, under refrigeration for up to seven
days.

USES
This makes a flavorful topping for steamed fresh vegetables.

MUSTARD VINIAGRETTE ♣

YIELD   5¼ CUPS

Cooks Notes

INGREDIENTS

1 Cup	Tarragon Vinegar
1 Cup	Country Dijon Mustard
3 Cups	Olive Oil
½ Cup	Sugar
1 tsp	Black Pepper - ground
2 Tbls	Chives

PREPARATION

In a mixing bowl, whisk vinegar and mustard together well. Add olive oil slowly, mixing well. Then add sugar and pepper, mixing well. Just prior to the use as a marinade or dressing add chives.

HINTS

This Viniagrette may be stored for up to 14 days under refrigeration.
It is always best to make dressings at least a day ahead of use, to allow the flavors to marry.

USES

Aside from use as a salad dressing, this Viniagrette makes a great marinade for fresh blanched vegetables. As a vegetable marinade simply pour over blanched, chilled vegetables; i.e. asparagus spears, cauliflower, or broccoli.

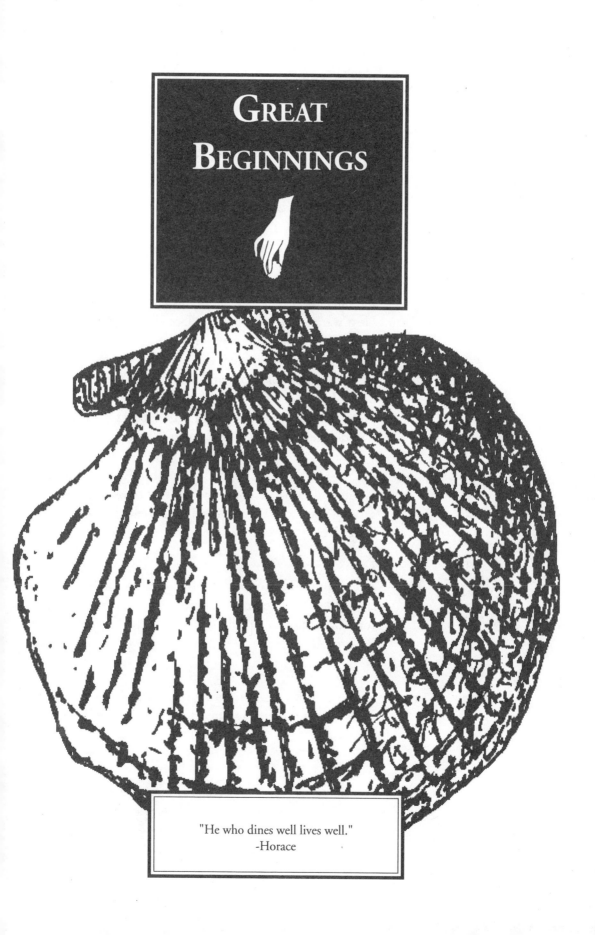

GREAT BEGINNINGS

"He who dines well lives well."
-Horace

Angels on Horseback

Yield   4 Servings

Cooks Notes

Ingredients

20	Oysters, medium size - shelled
2 Cups	Water
10 Strips	Bacon
20	Round wooden toothpicks
1 Cup	Bread Crumbs - finely chopped Δ
8 Tbls	Garlic Butter Sauce (Pg 45)
12 pieces	Pepperidge Farm Party Rye Cocktail Loaf

Preparation

Heat water nearly to boiling. Place oysters in water to blanch. Remove after one minute and set aside to cool. Cut strips of bacon in half to give 20 pieces. Wrap each oyster in a strip of bacon and secure with a toothpick through the center. Dredge these Angels through the bread crumbs, covering completely. Preheat the oven to 450 degrees. Place the Angels on a sheet pan and bake for 4 - 5 minutes or until golden brown. Spread bread pieces with 3 Tbl Garlic Butter Sauce, and broil. Melt remaining Garlic Butter Sauce. Place three pieces of bread on each serving plate, top with 5 Angels and melted Garlic Butter Sauce.

Hints

Δ This breading requires very fine bread crumbs. If 'Japanese style', i.e. coarse crumbs, are available, process for 1 or 2 minutes in a food processor to reduce the size of the crumb.

Variations

A traditional way of preparing the Angels is to use a flour and paprika mixture and to deep fry instead of baking.

SHERRY BUTTER SCALLOPS

YIELD   1 SERVING

INGREDIENTS   *Cooks Notes*

6   Nantucket Cape Scallops ◊1
1 Tbl   Dry Sherry
1 Tbl   Garlic Butter Sauce (Pg 45) ◊2
¼ Cup   Flour

PREPARATION

Dust scallops in flour and shake off all unnecessary flour.
In a sauté pan, heat Garlic Butter Sauce and sherry. Add
scallops, sautéing for 2 minutes. Place the scallops on a
broiler pan and place under the broiler for 2 - 3 minutes
until they are a light brown color.

VARIATIONS

◊1 The scallops you choose make the dish. We recommend the finest scallop in the world, the Nantucket Cape
Scallop, sometimes called Nantucket Bay Scallops. If the
Nantucket is not available, other northern bay scallops are
fine. Avoid southern scallops as their flavor leaves much to
be desired.
◊2 If garlic flavor is not desired, replace Garlic Butter
Sauce with regular butter.

USES

A triple portion, served with Rice Pilaf (Pg 92), makes an
excellent entree.

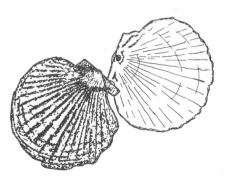

CAJUN SHRIMP

YIELD   4 SERVINGS

INGREDIENTS

24	Jumbo Shrimp - shell on Δ1
1 Tbl	Cajun Spice (Pg 50)
1 Tbl	Butter ◊

PREPARATION

Remove shrimp from shell Δ2 and lay on side. Butterfly the shrimp by carefully inserting sharp knife into the large end of the shrimp, cutting in about ¾ of the way to the back, then cutting to the tail. Be careful not to cut through the shrimp. Rinse the shrimp clean. On the stove, get a medium sauté pan VERY HOT. Melt butter in sauté pan, then add shrimp. Shake pan vigorously so that the shrimp will not stick. Sprinkle Cajun Spice on the shrimp and again shake the pan vigorously. Continue to cook over high heat until the shrimp are completely cooked, about 5 - 7 minutes, shaking while cooking to heat evenly and prevent scorching. When cooked, the center of the shrimp should have lost the raw, transparent appearance.

HINTS

Δ1 In the restaurant, we use what are called 21 x 25 Shrimp. This means 21 - 25 shrimp to the pound, and are jumbo shrimp. Another common size is 15 x 20, a bit larger, and as good for this recipe. If you find IQF (Individually Quick Frozen) shrimp with the shell on, buy it, do not buy cooked shrimp. If you find E-Z Peel shrimp, buy them - they have been cleaned and the shell will pull off easily, and are worth the extra cost.

Δ2 For the most professional looking dish, carefully leave tail on the shrimp when removing from the shell.

VARIATIONS

◊ Garlic Butter Sauce (Pg 45) may be substitited for the regular butter for even more flavor.

USES

This recipe serves two when used as an entree, and is particularly nice with Rice Pilaf (Pg 92).

PAN FRIED ALLIGATOR

YIELD   **10 SERVINGS**

INGREDIENTS

Cooks Notes

1 Lb	Alligator Meat Δ1
2 Cups	Herbal Breading (Pg 36)
2	Eggs
1 Cup	Water
½ Cup	Flour
10 Tbls	Butter
10 Tbls	Lemon Butter Sauce (Pg 44)
3 Tbls	Fresh Parsley - chopped

PREPARATION

Prepare egg wash by vigorously beating eggs and water together. Prepare alligator by cutting into silver dollar size pieces and pounding into thin pancakes with a kitchen mallet, being careful not to tear the meat apart. This pounding helps to tenderize the meat. Dust each piece of alligator in the flour, dip in egg wash Δ2, then dredge through the Herbal Breading, making sure that all sides are covered. Get a sauté pan VERY HOT. After melting butter in the pan, add alligator pieces and cook on each side 3 minutes or until golden brown. Serve each piece on a small plate topped with 1 Tbl Lemon Butter Sauce and a sprinkle of parsley.

HINTS

Δ1 Use farm raised alligator.
Δ2 When breading the alligator, use a two handed method. One hand remains dry and the other hand is used to dip the alligator into the egg wash. By doing this you will not end up with a pound of breading stuck to your fingers.

SMOKED CHUB PATÉ

YIELD   2 ½ CUPS

Cooks Notes

INGREDIENTS

1½ Lbs	Smoked Chubs ◊
½ Cup	Cream Cheese - softened
¼ Cup	Margarine - softened
1 tsp	Prepared Horseradish
¼ tsp	Tabasco Sauce

PREPARATION

Prepare the Chubs by skinning and carefully removing all bones, to yield about 1 pound of de-boned and skinned Chub. Then place in a food processor and process on medium high speed until reduced to a paste (this pulverizes any tiny Chub bones missed in the de-boning). Add softened cream cheese, softened margarine, horseradish and Tabasco sauce and mix well on medium low speed. Place in a sealable container, seal and chill.

HINTS

May be kept stored under refrigeration for a maximum of two weeks.

VARIATIONS

◊ Any smoked fish can be used if smoked Chubs are not available. Whitefish, Salmon, or Bluefish make a nice paté, and should be prepared without use of a food processor. Mix with an electric mixer or by hand to retain some of the texture of the fish.

CRAB STUFFED MUSHROOMS

YIELD   10 SERVINGS

INGREDIENTS

Cooks Notes

20	Large Button Mushrooms
½ Cup	Herbal Breading (Pg 36)
½ Cup	Sharp Cheddar Cheese - grated
½ Cup	Sour Cream
½ Cup	Crab Meat Stuffing (pg 39)
2 Tbls	Green Onions - chopped
1	Egg
1 Tbl	Light Soy Sauce
2 Tbls	Margarine - melted

PREPARATION

If mushrooms have stems, remove them and reserve. With a spoon, hollow out center of cap, then wash caps and drain well, patting dry Δ. Take ¼ cup of mushroom stems and finely chop. In a mixing bowl, add Herbal Breading, cheddar cheese, sour cream, Crab Meat Stuffing, green onion, egg, and soy sauce, and mix well. Brush the rounded end of the caps with melted margarine and stuff the cap with the mixture, rounding the top. Place stuffed side up in a baking dish or casserole and bake in a pre-heated oven at 350 degrees for 20 minutes.

HINTS

Δ Thoroughly drying the mushroom caps is essential to the integrity of the dish. Excess moisture will cause the mushroom to fall apart when baked.

VARIATIONS

To add a little color, sprinkle the top of the stuffed caps with paprika before serving.

OLIVE CHEESE BALL

YIELD   4 CUPS

Cooks Notes

INGREDIENTS

2 Cups	Cream Cheese - softened
¼ Cup	Margarine - softened
1 Cup	Green Olives - chopped
1 Cup	Black Olives - chopped
¼ Cup	Fresh Parsley - chopped

PREPARATION
Allow cream cheese and margarine 2 hours to soften at room temperature; drain olives ◊. Mix softened cream cheese, softened margarine, and both kinds of chopped olives carefully by hand. Form into a ball. Refrigerate until well chilled. Just before serving, roll into fresh parsley to coat the cheese ball, and serve.

HINTS
If you can't make this one, don't stand near a hot stove, or read any further in this book.

VARIATIONS
This takes on a different character if you roll the ball in chopped pecans or walnuts instead of parsley.
◊ Reserve a portion of liquid from the olives, and use to thin mixture to make a spread for party loaves, tea sandwiches, etc.

USES
Serve with crackers, when entertaining, as part of a brunch.

HUMMUS ♣

YIELD   3 CUPS

INGREDIENTS

3 Cups	Canned Garbanzo Beans (chick peas)
½ Cup	Water
½ Cup	Sesame Tahini Paste
¼ Cup	Fresh Lemon Juice
1 Tbl	Garlic Puree
¾ Tbl	Cumin - ground
1½ Tbls	Olive Oil
1 Tbl	Fresh Parsley - chopped
3	Pita Bread Pockets

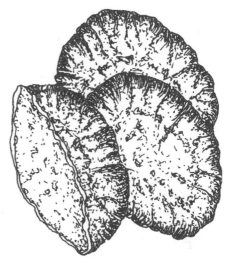

PREPARATION

In a food processor or blender, mix sesame tahini paste, lemon juice and garlic puree to a smooth paste. Add drained garbanzo beans and water and continue to mix until smooth, almost creamy. Add cumin. Δ ◊ Transfer mixture to a dinner plate and spread evenly, about ½ inch in thickness. Score the top with a fork, pour olive oil over and add fresh parsley. Split pita pockets and cut each into quarters. Broil for 1 - 2 minutes to dry and crisp pita chips. Serve pita chips as dippers with the Hummus.

HINTS

Δ Make Hummus mixture a day in advance of serving, and store under refrigeration.

VARIATIONS

◊ You may salt to taste. We don't find it necessary.

Spanakopeta

Yield   50 Pieces

Cooks Notes

Ingredients

10 oz Pkg	Frozen Spinach - finely chopped
¼ Cup	Cream Cheese - softened
¼ Cup	Feta Cheese
¼ Cup	Onion - finely chopped
1	Egg
2 tsp	Olive Oil
¼ tsp	Salt
¼ tsp	Dill Weed
¼ Lb	Butter - melted
17 sheets	Filo (phyllo) dough Δ1

Preparation

Thaw spinach, squeeze dry Δ2, finely chop. In a mixing bowl, combine softened cream cheese, feta cheese and onions, mixing well. Add spinach, lightly beaten egg, olive oil, salt and dill weed, mixing thoroughly.

Place one sheet of the filo dough Δ1 with the short end towards you. Brush with butter then fold in half away from you and brush again with butter. Cut the folded sheet into 3 equal strips. Place one tsp spinach mixture at the end of strip and fold corner over to make a triangle. Fold the dough over from side to side in the shape of a triangle to end of strip (see diagram). Repeat until all the spinach mixture has been used, then preheat oven to 350 degrees and bake on un-greased sheet pan for 20 minutes.

Cooks Notes

HINTS

Δ1 About filo dough:

This recipe uses only a small portion of the smallest traditional package of dough. Unused dough may be stored frozen, and will keep for up to a year; thaw completely before use.

Before working with filo dough, allow to sit out, covered, at room temperature for at least 2 hours.

While working have unused dough covered to keep moist.

Δ2 It is important that the spinach be as dry as possible. To dry spinach, place the spinach in the center of a kitchen towel, bring up the sides and twist the cloth to squeeze out excess moisture.

Unbaked Spanakopeta can be stored frozen in a sealed container and may be baked without thawing, allowing 3 - 5 minutes additional cooking time.

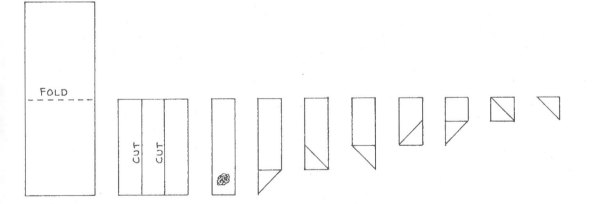

PARMESAN CHEESE PUFFS ♣

YIELD   64 ROUNDS

Cooks Notes

INGREDIENTS

1½ Cups	Parmesan Cheese - grated
1½ Cups	Margarine
1	Medium Onion - finely chopped
⅛ tsp	Cayenne Pepper
1 Loaf	Pepperidge Farm Original Bread

PREPARATION

A day ahead of time, mix cheese, margarine, onion, and cayenne pepper, and refrigerate in a sealed container. Using a round cookie cutter, about 1 inch diameter, cut rounds from bread, four to five rounds per slice. Toast in 350 degree oven for 10 minutes or until slightly golden. Before serving spread the toasted rounds with the cheese mixture and broil for 1 - 2 minutes. Watch the broiling procedure closely so as not to over cook and burn.

SOUPS, SALADS & SIDE DISHES

"If a fool be associated with a man all his life
he will perceive the truth as little as a spoon
perceives the taste of soup."
-Buddha

CHILLED CHERRY SOUP ♣

YIELD   5 CUPS

Cooks Notes

INGREDIENTS

100 Large	Pitted Tart Cherries Δ1
2½ Cups	Water
7½ tsp	Sugar
5	2" Cinnamon Sticks
1	Lemon - entire peel
10 Tbls	Rosé Wine
5 tsp	Corn Starch
1¼ Cups	Low - Fat Yogurt

PREPARATION

In a small saucepan, combine cherries, water, sugar, cinnamon stick and lemon peel. Bring to a boil. Reduce heat, cover and simmer for 20 minutes. Remove and discard cinnamon stick and lemon peel from the cherry mixture. In a separate bowl, combine rosé wine and cornstarch Δ2; stirring to dissolve cornstarch, then add to cherry mixture, stirring constantly, and bring back to boil. Reduce heat and simmer until mixture thickens. In a mixing bowl, stir yogurt until smooth; add cherry mixture and stir to combine. Cover and refrigerate until well chilled Δ3. Serve in a soup cup, topped with 1 Tbl yogurt, a fresh cherry and mint leaf.

HINTS

Δ1 We use IQF (Individually Quick Frozen) Leelanau County tart cherries, and simply count out 100.
Δ2 To improve mixing, add wine to corn starch, rather than corn starch to wine.
Δ3 It is best to hold chilled overnight.

SWISS ONION SOUP

YIELD   5 CUPS

INGREDIENTS

Cooks Notes

2 Cups	Water
5 Tbls	Butter
1 tsp	Garlic Puree
3 Cups	Onion - thinly sliced
¾ tsp	Dry Mustard
½ tsp	Salt
3 Tbls	Flour
1½ Cups	Milk - scalded
1½ Cups	Swiss Cheese - shredded
½ tsp	Prepared Horseradish
1 Tbl	Dry Sherry
½ tsp	Black Pepper - ground
½ tsp	Soy Sauce
3 Drops	Tabasco Sauce
2 Shakes	Worcestershire Sauce

PREPARATION

In a saucepan, combine water, 2 Tbls butter, garlic puree, onion slices, mustard and salt; cover and simmer over low heat, until onions are tender, about 20 minutes. Scald milk. In a separate saucepan, make a roux by melting remaining 3 Tbl butter and stirring in flour, cooking while stirring over low heat for 5 minutes. Add scalded milk to roux Δ, mixing well to make a medium thick cream sauce. Then slowly add shredded cheese to sauce, mixing until melted. Add horseradish and sherry to cheese sauce and combine the cheese sauce with contents of saucepan containing onions, mixing thoroughly. Mix in pepper, soy, Tabasco and worcestershire sauces.

HINTS

Δ Scalded milk must be hot when added to the roux, to make cream sauce thicken quickly.
This soup may be stored frozen, sealed, for 2 -3 months.

USES

This soup makes a fine base for creamy pasta sauces, for example, Scandinavian Seafood Pasta (Pg 154).

CHILLED BEET SOUP ❧

YIELD   6 CUPS

INGREDIENTS

3 Lb	New Beets - small, with leaves
12 Cups	Water
8 tsp	Wyler's Chicken Bouillon
1 Bunch	Scallions
8 Tbls	Sour Cream
1 Tbl	Fresh Dill - chopped
2	Lemons - zest only

PREPARATION

Trim the beets, leaving 2 inches of the stems and the root ends attached to prevent bleeding, reserving the leaves. Wash trimmed beets and reserved leaves thoroughly. Cut scallions in half lengthwise. In a soup pot, combine bouillon and water, add beets, leaves and scallions. Bring to a boil then reduce heat and simmer until beets are tender. Turn off heat and remove beets from pot. Under cold running water, remove skins and stems from beets, then cut beets into a fine julienne. Strain the broth from the soup pot into a bowl, discarding the solids, then add the julienne beets to the bowl. Refrigerate until thoroughly chilled Δ. Serve in soup bowl, topped with 1 Tbl sour cream and fresh dill and lemon zest.

HINTS

Δ The soup is best made a day ahead of time, and can be kept under refrigeration for up to 2 weeks.

New England Clam Chowder

Yield   20 Cups

Ingredients

1 Qt	Fresh Steamer Clams - shucked Δ
4 Large	Onions - sliced
2 Stalks	Celery - diced ¼ inch
4 Cups	Water
6 Cups	Raw Potatoes - diced ¼ inch
4 tsp	Salt
½ tsp	Black Pepper - ground
2	Bay Leaves
1 tsp	Fresh Parsley - chopped
½ tsp	Thyme Leaf
1 Tbl	Worcestershire Sauce
2 Cups	Half & Half - scalded
4 Cups	Milk - scalded
3 Cups	Clam Juice
2 Tbls	Flour
6 Tbls	Butter

Preparation

In a large soup pot, melt 3 Tbl butter, add sliced onions and diced celery, sauté until onions are golden brown. Then add water, diced potatoes, clams, salt, pepper, bay leaves, chopped parsley, thyme, worcestershire sauce. Bring to a boil, then reduce the heat, and cook gently for 15 - 20 minutes, until the potatoes are tender. Meanwhile, scald half & half and milk. Reserve two cups broth from soup pot, then add scalded half & half, scalded milk and clam juice to soup pot. In a sauté pan make a roux by melting remaining butter, stirring in flour, mixing well, and cooking about one minute, using care not to burn Add reserved broth to roux, mix well and add to soup pot, mixing well and simmering for 15 - 20 minutes.

Hints

Δ For this recipe, use of canned clams is discouraged, as the quality of the chowder will be severely diminished. If you do not know how to shuck fresh steamer clams, buy them shucked or get someone who does know how to shuck them to do it for you, to ensure the removal of the sand sack.

CAPE BLUEFISH CHOWDER

YIELD   6 SERVINGS

INGREDIENTS

3 Lb	Cape Bluefish, whole-dressed ◊
3 Cups	Water
1 tsp	Salt
1 tsp	Thyme Leaf
1 Large	Onion - thinly sliced
1 Large	Carrot - thinly sliced
2 Large	Russett Potatoes - peeled & diced
2 Cups	Whole Milk
2 Cups	Half & Half
¼ Cup	Butter - softened
¼ Cup	Flour
	Salt & Pepper to Taste
3 Tbls	Butter - softened
1 Tbl	Fresh Chives - chopped

PREPARATION

Remove and skin fillets, reserving for chowder. Place head, skin and bones in a large saucepan. Add water, salt, thyme, sliced onion and sliced carrot. Bring to a boil, then reduce heat and simmer, covered, for 20 minutes. Strain and return broth, onions and carrots to saucepan. Add diced potatoes, cover and simmer for 15 minutes, or until potatoes are tender. Preheat and stir in milk and half & half. In a separate bowl, mix ¼ Cup butter and flour into a paste. Add to chowder, stirring until paste is melted and chowder thickens slightly. Cut reserved fillets into 1 inch cubes and add to chowder. Simmer for 15 minutes. Season with salt and pepper. Serve in chowder bowl (a deep soup bowl), topping each bowl with ½ Tbl of butter and a sprinkle of chives, and alongside chowder crackers.

VARIATIONS

◊ Any firm - textured, flavorful fish may be substituted for Cape Bluefish; for example, Sea Bass, Grouper, Red Snapper, etc.

Greek Salad ♣

Yield   4 Servings

Ingredients

1 Large Head	Iceburg Lettuce
1 Large Head	Red Leaf Lettuce
8 Tbls	Feta Cheese
16	Greek Olives - whole
8	Sliced Beets - julienned
8-12	Thin Slices Red Onion
½ Cup	Greek Dressing (Pg 58)

Cooks Notes

Preparation
Wash and dry the lettuces Δ. Hand tear the lettuces into a large salad bowl and mix well. Sprinkle feta cheese, Greek olives and julienned beets on the lettuces, finally laying thinly sliced red onion atop the salad. At the table before serving, toss with Greek Dressing.

Hints
Δ Dressings will not stick to wet lettuce. Always be certain the lettuce is dry, by draining for several hours, spinning dry, or carefully patting with a dry towel.

Caesar Salad

Yield   4 Servings

Ingredients

1 Large Head	Romaine Lettuce
8 Tbls	Romano Cheese - grated ◊
1 Cup	Croutons
4 Fillets	Canned Anchovy
⅓ Cup	Caesar Dressing (Pg 59)

Preparation

Chill 4 serving plates. Wash and dry the lettuce Δ. Tear each romaine leaf into 3 or 4 pieces and place in large salad (or mixing) bowl. Add Ceasar Dressing and 4 Tbl Romano cheese, mixing thoroughly to coat all sides of lettuce leaves. To serve, divide lettuce among 4 chilled plates, allowing leaves to fall onto the plates for height. Sprinkle each serving with 1 Tbl Romano cheese and top with anchovy fillet and ¼ cup croutons.

Hints

Δ Dressings will not stick to wet lettuce. Always be certain the lettuce is dry, by draining for several hours, spinning dry, or carefully patting with a dry towel.

Variations

◊ The 'bite' of the salad may be changed using a mixture of Romano and Parmesan cheeses.

INN SALAD ♣

YIELD   4 SERVINGS

INGREDIENTS   *Cooks Notes*

1 Large Head	Bibb Lettuce
1 Large Head	Red Leaf Lettuce
2 Tbls	Sunflower Seeds
2 Tbls	Blue Cheese - crumbled
8 - 12	Thin Slices of Red Onion
½ Cup	Raspberry Viniagrette Dressing (Pg 60)

PREPARATION
Wash and dry the lettuces Δ. Hand tear the lettuces into a
large chilled salad bowl and mix well. Sprinkle sunflower
seeds and blue cheese on the lettuces, finally laying thinly
sliced red onion atop the salad. At the table, before
serving, toss with Raspberry Vinaigrette Dressing.

HINTS
Δ Dressings will not stick to wet lettuce. Always be certain
the lettuce is dry, by draining for several hours, spinning
dry, or carefully patting with a dry towel.

87

Marinated Tomatoes ♣

Yield   8 Servings

Cooks Notes

Ingredients

3 Large	Ripe Garden Tomatoes ◊
⅓ Cup	Olive Oil
¼ Cup	Red Wine Vinegar
¼ tsp	White Pepper - ground
½ tsp	Garlic Puree
2 Tbls	Sugar
2 Tbls	Onions - finely chopped
1 Tbl	Basil Leaf
1 Tbl	Fresh Parsley - finely chopped

Preparation

Peel and thickly slice tomatoes and place in a large shallow dish. In a mixing bowl, combine olive oil, wine vinegar, pepper, garlic puree, sugar, chopped onions, basil, and parsley, mixing well. Pour mixture over tomatoes, cover and refrigerate for several hours before serving.

Variations

◊ You may use any favorite fresh garden vegetable in place of or in addition to tomatoes.

Adding ¼ Cup Country Dijon Mustard makes a creamy, spiced marinade - particularly flavorful with fresh lightly blanched asparagus spears.

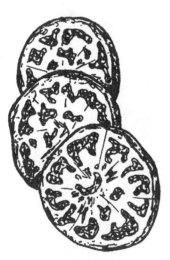

Stewed Tomatoes

Yield   4 Servings

Ingredients

Cooks Notes

5 Large	Ripe Garden Tomatoes
3 Tbls	Canola Oil
1 Cup	Onion - thinly sliced
1 tsp	Garlic Puree
½ tsp	Basil Leaf
½ tsp	Whole Oregano

Preparation

Place tomatoes in a pot and cover with water. Bring to a boil, and cook until tomato skins begin to split. Remove tomatoes from hot water, and plunge into cold water bath. Peel skins from tomatoes and set tomatoes aside. Place one tomato in blender and puree. Preheat oven to 350 degrees. In a sauté pan, heat oil and add sliced onions, garlic puree, basil and oregano and sauté until very tender but not browned, then add tomato puree. Place skinned tomatoes in a serving casserole dish, top with sautéed onion mixture, cover and bake in 350 degree oven for 15 - 20 minutes.

Hints

This may seem like a lot of work, when one could open a can of stewed tomatoes, heat and serve. The flavor of these stewed tomatoes, however, is worth the extra effort.

ACORN SQUASH

YIELD   2 CUPS

INGREDIENTS

2 - 1 Lb	Acorn Squash Δ ◊
½ Cup	Butter - melted
3 Tbls	Brown Sugar
½ tsp	Salt
¼ tsp	White Pepper - ground
¼ tsp	Nutmeg - ground
½ tsp	Cinnamon - ground

PREPARATION

Cut each squash in half and remove seeds. Place cut side down in a pan with about ¼ inch of water and cover with foil. Cook at 400 degrees for 30 minutes, or until tender. Allow to cool after cooking; remove skin, and place cooked squash pulp in a mixing bowl. Add butter, 2 Tbls brown sugar, salt, pepper, nutmeg and cinnamon, mix well. Place in casserole dish and bake, covered, for 20 minutes at 350 degrees. Remove the cover, sprinkle remaining brown sugar on top and bake uncovered another 5 minutes.

HINTS

Δ This is a small size acorn squash. We use this size because we feel the flavor is superior to that of larger squash.

VARIATIONS

◊ Other small fall squash, such as butternut or buttercup may be used as well.

Baked Spinach

Yield   3 Cups

Ingredients

Cooks Notes

2 - 10 oz Pkgs	Frozen Chopped Spinach
2½ tsp	Flour
3 Tbls	Butter
2 Tbls	Clam Juice
2 Tbls	White Table Wine
½ Tbl	Tomato Paste
⅛ tsp	Salt
⅛ tsp	White Pepper - ground
⅓ Cup	Half & Half
½ Cup	Cream Cheese - softened
2	Green Onions - diced
1 Tbl	Fresh Lemon Juice
¼ Cup	Bread Crumbs
¼ Cup	Romano Cheese - grated ◊

Preparation

Thaw spinach and place in a medium size casserole dish.
In a separate saucepan, make a roux by melting 1 Tbl
butter and stirring in flour, cooking while stirring over
low heat for 5 minutes. Stir in clam juice and wine and
cook for 5 minutes on low heat. Add the tomato paste,
salt & pepper and half & half and cook for 8 minutes on
low heat. Mix in softened cream cheese, remaining butter,
diced green onions and lemon juice; heat thoroughly.
Pour the mixture over the spinach, top with bread crumbs
and Romano cheese. Bake at 350 degrees, uncovered, for
30 minutes, until bubbling.

Variations

◊ Any grated hard cheese may be substituted; for example,
Parmesan or asiago.

RICE PILAF

YIELD   4 CUPS

Cooks Notes

INGREDIENTS

1½ Cup	Long Grain White Rice ◊1
3 Cups	Water
1½ tsp	Wyler's Chicken Bouillon
1½ tsp	Wyler's Beef Bouillon
6 Tbls	Butter
¼ Cup	Onions - finely chopped ◊2

PREPARATION

In a small mixing bowl, combine chicken & beef bouillon with water, mix well and set aside. In a sauté pan, melt 3 Tbls butter, add chopped onions and sauté until tender. Preheat oven to 375 degrees. In a large casserole dish, place uncooked rice, add sautéed onions and mix well Δ. Add bouillon and water mixture, mix well, bring to a boil on stove. Then cover with foil, cut two or three slits in the foil and bake 18 minutes at 375 degrees. Remove foil and mix in the remaining butter.

HINTS

Δ To assure an even mixture of onions and rice, add bouillion and water mixture only after pre-mixing rice and onions.

VARIATIONS

◊1 Brown rice may be substituted for white rice, or a mixture of wild and brown or white rices will produce an interesting pilaf.

◊2 Shallots and/or Leeks may be substituted for the onions.

To spice up this rice add a touch of sherry to the bouillon/ water mixture.

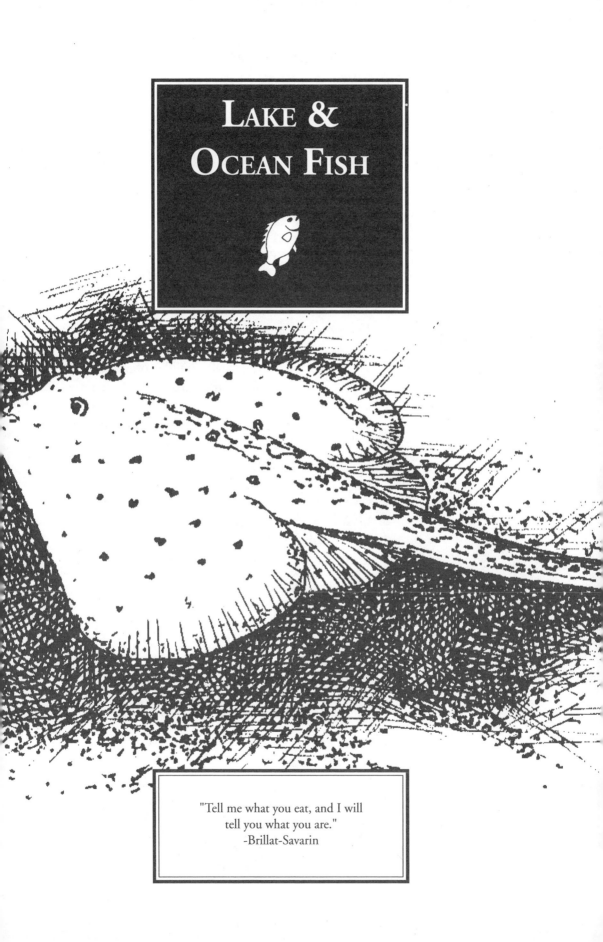

LAKE & OCEAN FISH

"Tell me what you eat, and I will
tell you what you are."
-Brillat-Savarin

PAN FRIED LAKE PERCH ♣

YIELD   4 SERVINGS

INGREDIENTS

24 Fillets	Lake Perch Fillets - fresh or frozen ◊1
2 Cups	Milk
1/2 tsp	Paprika
¼ Cup	Butter
¼ Cup	Dry Sherry
½ Cup	Flour
½ Cup	Lemon Butter Sauce (Pg 44)
2 Tbls	Fresh Parsley - chopped

PREPARATION

If frozen fillets are used, thaw. Be sure fillets are free from scales and bones. In a small sealable container place milk and layer fillets into the milk so all of the fillets are covered. Seal and refrigerate at least 24 hours Δ. Drain milk and discard, leaving fillets moist. In a sauté pan, melt butter, and get very hot, without burning. Lightly dredge fillets in flour - do not thickly coat with flour ◊2. Place fillets in the sauté pan skin side up, immediately add sherry around, not over, fillets and cook until golden brown, turning fillets to brown on each side. Top each six fillet serving with 2 Tbls Lemon Butter Sauce and sprinkle with fresh parsley.

HINTS

Δ The milk keeps fresh fillets moist and returns moisture to frozen fillets prior to cooking. You may store fillets in milk for 2 or 3 days (be sure to check the expiration date of the milk prior to usage so that it does not sour). This is a useful technique for frozen poultry and meat as well.

VARIATIONS

◊1 If Lake Perch is not available, several fresh lake and ocean fish are excellent pan fried with this Lemon Butter Sauce, including Trout, Pickerel, Walleye, Whitefish, Salmon, Cape Bluefish, Schrod, Sole, Monkfish and many others.
◊2 Add either Almondine Breading or Herbal Breading to make a heartier dish. Refer to Sole Almondine (Pg 102) for breading procedure.
◊ Add 1 Tbl pecan pieces to make Lemon Pecan Butter Sauce.

SUGGESTED WINES

dry, light or medium white:
Good Harbor Chardonnay

OR

semi-dry, light or medium white:
L. Mawby PGW Pun

SUGGESTED DINNER MENU

Crab Stuffed Mushrooms (Pg 73)

Wild Rice Salad (Pg 188)

Pan Fried Lake Perch

Stewed Tomatoes (Pg 89)

Peanut Butter Pie (Pg 216)

BROILED WHITEFISH WITH LEMON BUTTER SAUCE

Cooks Notes

YIELD   4 SERVINGS

INGREDIENTS

4 - 10 oz	Fresh Whitefish Fillets Δ1 ◊
½ tsp	Paprika
½ tsp	Canola Oil
¼ Cup	Lemon Butter Sauce (Pg 44)
2 Tbls	Fresh Parsley - chopped

PREPARATION

If necessary, remove pin bones from fillets (see Pg 34 for instructions). Place the fillets on a broiling pan and sprinkle with paprika, then brush with oil and place in the broiler Δ2. Broil until fully cooked Δ3, about 7 - 8 minutes. Remove from broiler, place on serving plate and top each fillet with 1 Tbl Lemon Butter Sauce and sprinkle with chopped parsley.

HINTS

Δ1 The importance of quality fresh fish cannot be over emphasized. The difference between a superb fish dinner and an ordinary dinner begins with the quality and freshness of the fish.

Δ2 Have the fillets at least 3 inches from broiler.

Δ3 A fillet is fully cooked when the outside is golden brown and the center of the fillet has lost its translucent appearance and is nearly white.

VARIATIONS

◊ If fresh Whitefish is not available, several fresh lake and ocean fish are excellent broiled with this Lemon Butter Sauce, including Lake Trout, Pickerel, Walleye, Perch, Salmon, Cape Bluefish, Schrod, Sole, Monkfish and many others.

SUGGESTED WINES

dry, medium or heavy white:
Boskydel Vignoles

OR

semi-dry, medium white:
Good Harbor Trillium

SUGGESTED DINNER MENU

Swiss Onion Soup (Pg 81)

Inn Salad (Pg 87)

Broiled Whitefish

Gourmet Potatoes (Pg 194)

Chocolate Raspberry Cheesecake (Pg 222)

WHITEFISH NEPTUNE

YIELD   4 SERVINGS

Cooks Notes

INGREDIENTS

4 - 10 oz	Fresh Whitefish Fillets Δ ◊1
2 Cups	Crab Meat Stuffing (Pg 39)
½ tsp	Paprika ◊2
½ tsp	Canola Oil
½ Cup	Bearnaise Sauce (Pg 54) ◊3
2 Tbls	Fresh Parsley - chopped

PREPARATION

If necessary, remove pin bones from fillets (see Pg 34 for instructions). Preheat oven to 375 degrees. Place the fillets on a baking pan. Lay ½ cup Crab Meat Stuffing on the top of each fillet and shape to the fillet, covering about ¾ of the fillet. Press the stuffing into place and sprinkle fillet and stuffing with paprika. Brush oil on the stuffed fillets and bake in preheated oven for 20 minutes. Remove from oven and place each fillet on a dinner plate and top each with 2 Tbls Bearnaise Sauce. Sprinkle chopped parsley on fillets and serve.

HINTS

Δ The importance of quality fresh fish cannot be over emphasized. The difference between a superb fish dinner and an ordinary dinner begins with the quality and freshness of the fish.

VARIATIONS

◊1 If fresh Whitefish is not available, several fresh lake and ocean fish are excellent stuffed and baked, including Lake Trout, Pickerel, Walleye, Salmon, Schrod and Sole.
◊2 To add spice, you may replace paprika with Cajun Spice (Pg 50).
◊3 Instead of Bearnaise Sauce, Lemon Butter Sauce, with or without pecans, may be used.

SUGGESTED WINES

dry, medium or heavy white:
Leelanau Chardonnay

OR

dry, medium rosé:
Boskydel Rosé de Chaunac

SUGGESTED DINNER MENU

New England Clam Chowder (Pg 83)

Caesar Salad (Pg 86)

Whitefish Neptune

Stewed Tomatoes (Pg 89)

Creme Caramel (Pg 211)

99

Blackened Whitefish

Yield   4 Servings

Cooks Notes

Ingredients

4 - 10 oz	Fresh Whitefish Fillets Δ1 ◊
½ Cup	Cajun Spice (Pg 50)
½ Cup	Butter
4 Medallions	Pecan Butter Sauce (Pg 47)
2 Tbls	Fresh Parsley - chopped

Preparation

If necessary, remove pin bones from fillets (see Pg 34 for instructions). Cover both sides of each fillet with Cajun Spice, varying the quantity used on each fillet to adjust the spiciness of the dish to personal taste. Melt butter in preheated Δ2 iron skillet, allowing to brown. Lay fillets skin side up in the skillet. Cook fillets 4 minutes prior to turning. Turn fillets and cook 3 minutes, then remove from skillet and place each fillet on dinner plate, top each with a medallion of Pecan Butter Sauce, sprinkle with chopped parsley, and serve.

HINTS

Δ1 The importance of quality fresh fish cannot be over emphasized. The difference between a superb fish dinner and an ordinary dinner begins with the quality and freshness of the fish.

Δ2 For the best blackened fish use a black iron skillet. The skillet must be EXTREMELY HOT before use, in order to sear the fillets.

VARIATIONS

◊ If fresh Whitefish is not available, several fresh lake and ocean fish are excellent blackened in this way including Lake Trout, Pickerel, Walleye, Salmon, Cape Bluefish, Schrod, Monkfish, Mako Shark, Yellowfin Tuna, Swordfish and many others.

SUGGESTED WINES

dry, medium white:
Boskydel Soleil Blanc

OR

dry, sparkling:
L. Mawby Brut

SUGGESTED DINNER MENU

Cape Bluefish Chowder
(Pg 84)

Marinated Tomatoes
(Pg 88)

Blackened Whitefish

Baked Spinach (Pg 91)

Chocolate Raspberry
Brownies (Pg 224)

SOLE ALMONDINE

YIELD   4 SERVINGS

Cooks Notes

INGREDIENTS

4 - 8 oz	Fresh Lemon Sole Fillets Δ1 ◊
1 Cup	Almondine Breading (Pg 37)
2	Eggs
¾ Cup	Water
½ Cup	Flour
½ Cup	Butter
½ Cup	Lemon Butter Sauce (Pg 44)
2 Tbls	Fresh Parsley - chopped

PREPARATION

Prepping the fillet

With Lemon Sole fillets, and most other sole fillets, there are usually no bones to be concerned with; however, always take the time to inspect fillets to insure that they are boneless. In a small mixing bowl, mix egg and water together to make an egg wash. Place flour in a shallow pan and arrange fillets to the left of the flour, egg wash to the right. Place Almondine Breading in a shallow pan to the right of the egg wash. Δ2 Prepare fillets by dredging through flour, dusting off extra flour, then dipping in egg wash and placing in breading and coating both sides of fillet with breading. As each fillet is breaded, place in the refrigerator to hold prior to cooking. Preheat sauté pan, add butter, melt and get hot, without burning. Place fillets in hot butter and cook on each side until golden brown, about 3 minutes a side. To serve, place each fillet on a dinner plate and top each with 2 Tbls Lemon Butter Sauce and sprinkle with chopped parsley.

HINTS

Δ1 The importance of quality fresh fish cannot be over emphasized. The difference between a superb fish dinner and an ordinary dinner begins with the quality and freshness of the fish.

Δ2 When breading the fillets use a two handed method. One hand remains dry and the other hand is used to dip the fillets into the egg wash. By doing this you will not end up with a pound of breading stuck to your fingers.

VARIATIONS

◊ If fresh Sole is not available, several fresh lake and ocean fish are excellent with this breading, including Whitefish, Lake Trout, Pickerel, Walleye, Perch, Salmon, Schrod, Monkfish and many others.

SUGGESTED WINES

dry, medium or heavy white:
Good Harbor Pinot Gris

OR

semi-dry, light or medium white:
Leelanau Winter White

SUGGESTED DINNER MENU

Angels on Horseback (Pg 68)

Cajun Shrimp (Pg 70)

Sole Almondine

Corn Casserole (Pg 193)

Chocolate Filled Meringue Tarts (Pg 212)

CHAR GRILLED SALMON WITH BEARNAISE SAUCE

Cooks Notes

YIELD   4 SERVINGS

INGREDIENTS

4 - 8 oz	Salmon Steaks or Fillets Δ1 ◊
¼ Cup	Canola Oil
½ Cup	Bearnaise Sauce (Pg 54)
2 Tbls	Fresh Parsley - chopped

PREPARATION

If necessary, remove pin bones from fillets (see Pg 34 for instructions). Cooking will be done on an open flame char grill, preheated so that the rack is HOT. This will sear the fillet so that the meat should not stick to the rack. Brush both sides of fillets with oil and lay on the grill rack. Cook on uncovered Δ2 grill 2 minutes then rotate fillet 90 degrees and cook another 2 mintues, then turn fillet over, cook 2 minutes, rotate 90 degrees, and cook another 2 minutes. This procedure produces a nice 'checker board' of grill lines on the fillet. After 8 minutes total cooking time Δ3, remove the fish from grill, place each fillet on a dinner plate, top each with 2 Tbls Bearnaise Sauce, sprinkle with chopped parsley, and serve.

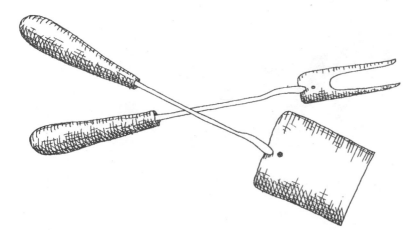

HINTS

Δ1 The importance of quality fresh fish cannot be over emphasized. The difference between a superb fish dinner and an ordinary dinner begins with the quality and freshness of the fish.

Δ2 Cooking on a covered grill will shorten cooking times given.

Δ3 Salmon tends to be a dry fish: it is important not to over cook the fillet. If your grill is cooking hot and the Salmon starts to get too dark, reduce cooking time.

VARIATIONS

◊ The char grilling procedure can be used with any steak cut fish; or with firm fillet fish, such as Sturgeon, White-fish or Halibut. Some fillets of fish, like Sole and Schrod, are so tender that they break apart on the grill and should not be used. A rule of thumb is that if the fillet is solid and firm it should stand up to the grill.

SUGGESTED WINES

dry, medium to heavy white:
L. Mawby Vignoles

OR

dry, light to medium red:
Good Harbor Coastal Red

SUGGESTED DINNER MENU

Sherry Butter Scallops (Pg 69)

Greek Salad (Pg 85)

Char Grilled Salmon

Rice Pilaf (Pg 92)

Heavenly Angel Pie (Pg 225)

BAKED SALMON ENCRUTE

YIELD 4 SERVINGS

INGREDIENTS

4 - 6 oz	Salmon Fillets Δ1 ◊1
¼ Cup	Carrots - julienned
¼ Cup	Mushrooms - sliced
¼ Cup	Onions - sliced
¼ Cup	Broccoli - florets
1 Box	Pepperidge Farm Puff Pastry Sheets Δ2
1	Egg
2 Tbls	Water
½ Cup	Bearnaise Sauce (Pg 54)
2 Tbls	Fresh Parsley - chopped

PREPARATION

If necessary, remove pin bones from fillets (see Pg 34 for instructions). ◊2 Remove skin from fillets. In a small mixing bowl, mix thoroughly julienned carrots, sliced mushrooms, sliced onions and broccoli florets ◊3. Cut each puff pastry sheet into four equal rectangles, making eight pieces. Place each fillet on a piece of the pastry, cover fillet with ¼ cup vegetable mixture, then lay another pastry piece over fillet and vegetables, pulling sides and ends to meet lower piece of pastry. Then, fold the lower piece of pastry over the top piece and pinch edges shut. Be sure that entire edge is sealed prior to cooking. In a small mixing bowl, make an egg wash by mixing egg and water together, then brush the top of the EnCrute with egg wash. Preheat a convection oven Δ3 to 325 degrees, place EnCrutes on baking pan treated with non-stick spray, and cook for 20 minutes. To serve, place each EnCrute on a dinner plate, top each with 2 Tbls Bearnaise Sauce and sprinkle with chopped parsley.

Hints

Δ1 The importance of quality fresh fish cannot be over emphasized. The difference between a superb fish dinner and an ordinary dinner begins with the quality and freshness of the fish.

Δ2 This puff pastry can be found at many food stores, in the freezer section. One box contains 2 sheets, each 14 inches by 11 inches.

Δ3 This dish is best when cooked in a convection oven. If a convection oven is not available, cook in a preheated conventional oven at 375 degrees for 20 minutes. To achieve a golden brown color, it may be necessary to broil for 1 - 2 minutes.

Variations

◊1 If fresh Salmon is not available, several fresh lake and ocean fish are excellent baked EnCrute including Lake Trout, Halibut, Haddock, Sole, Schrod, Monkfish and many others.

◊2 If you desire some additional flavors, prepare poaching stock by combining 2 cups water, 1 bay leaf, 4 pepper-corns, 2 Tbls white table wine. In a shallow covered pan, bring poaching stock to a boil, add fillets, skin on, and poach for 4 minutes, then remove skin, chill fillets and proceed as above.

◊3 You may substitute any of your favorite fresh veg-etables in the vegetable mix.

Suggested Wines

dry, medium to heavy white:
Boskydel Vignoles

OR

semi-dry, light to medium red:
Good Harbor Harbor Red

Suggested Dinner Menu

Hummus (Pg 75)

Inn Salad (Pg 87)

Baked Salmon EnCrute

Lemon Bread (Pg 210)

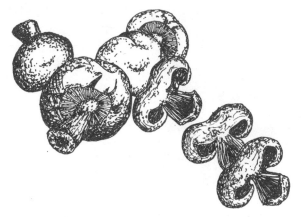

FISH IN A BAG

YIELD   4 SERVINGS

Cooks Notes

INGREDIENTS

4 - 8 oz	Fresh Haddock Fillets Δ1 ◊1
¼ Cup	Carrots - julienned
¼ Cup	Mushrooms - sliced
¼ Cup	Pea Pods
¼ Cup	Broccoli - florets
2 Sheets	Bakers Sheet Paper Δ2
¼ Cup	Water
4 tsp	Clam Juice
1 tsp	Garlic Puree
4 tsp	Canola Oil
2 Tbls	Fresh Parsley - chopped

PREPARATION

With Haddock fillets, there are usually no bones to be concerned with; however, always take the time to inspect fillets to insure that they are boneless. In a small mixing bowl, mix thoroughly julienned carrots, sliced mushrooms, pea pods and broccoli florets. ◊2 Preheat oven to 375 degrees. Prepare bags by cutting each sheet of bakers paper in half lengthwise (Fig. 1), then fold each piece in half to crease, then lay open (Fig. 2). Place each fillet on a piece of paper next to the crease (Fig. 3), cover each fillet with ¼ of the fresh vegetable mixture. Mix water, clam juice, garlic puree, oil and parsley together. Pour ¼ of the mixture on the top of each fillet. Fold sheet paper over fillet, folding the edges tightly together (Fig. 4), making certain the bag is sealed. Place bagged fillets in shallow baking pan, and bake in preheated oven for 18 minutes. Remove from oven, place each bag on a separate dinner plate and take to table, still bagged. At the table, cut the folded edge of the paper, pull paper away from fillet, and serve.

HINTS

Δ1 The importance of quality fresh fish cannot be over emphasized. The difference between a superb fish dinner and an ordinary dinner begins with the quality and freshness of the fish.

Δ2 Bakers sheet paper can be found at most food stores: 16½ inch x 24½ inch is the standard size that we use at the Inn.

VARIATIONS

◊1 If fresh Haddock is not available, several fresh lake and ocean fish are excellent baked in a bag including Lake Trout, Whitefish, Halibut, Sole, Schrod, Monkfish and many others.

◊2 You may substitute any of your favorite fresh vegetables in the vegetable mix.

SUGGESTED WINES

semi-dry, medium to heavy white:
L. Mawby Sandpiper

OR

dry, light to medium red:
Leelanau Autumn Harvest

SUGGESTED DINNER MENU

Smoked Chub Paté (Pg 72)

Chilled Fruit Salad (Pg 189)

Fish in a Bag

White Chocolate Mousse (Pg 215)

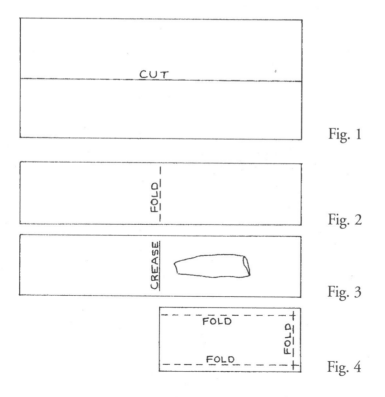

Fig. 1

Fig. 2

Fig. 3

Fig. 4

BLUEFISH WITH MUSTARD BUTTER

YIELD   4 SERVINGS

Cooks Notes

INGREDIENTS

2 Lbs	Fresh Cape Bluefish Fillets ◊
¼ Cup	White Table Wine
3 Cups	Water
¾ Cup	Lemon Juice
3⅓ Cups	Mustard Butter (Pg 46)
2 Tbls	Fresh Parsley - chopped

PREPARATION

Skin the fillets. In a dish large enough for the four fillets to lay flat, mix lemon juice, wine and water. Lay fillets in the mixture and marinate for 20 minutes. Remove fillets and place on a broiler pan. Generously coat one side of the fillets with the mustard butter, using 1½ cups. Place under the broiler about 4 inches from the heat and cook for 6 minutes. Carefully turn fillets and generously coat the other side, using 1½ cups Mustard Butter, returning to broiler for an additional 6 minutes. In a small sauce pan, heat remaining Mustard Butter. Remove fillets, place each on a dinner plate, pour melted Mustard Butter over, sprinkle with chopped parsley, and serve.

HINTS

Δ The importance of quality fresh fish cannot be over emphasized. The difference between a superb fish dinner and an ordinary dinner begins with the quality and freshness of the fish.

VARIATIONS

◊ If fresh Bluefish is not available, several fresh lake and ocean fish are excellent with Mustard Butter including Lake Trout, Salmon, Sturgeon, Tuna, Monkfish and many others.

SUGGESTED WINES

dry, medium white:
Good Harbor Chardonnay

OR

dry, light to medium red:
Boskydel DeChaunac

SUGGESTED DINNER MENU

Pan Fried Alligator (Pg 71)

Wild Rice Salad (Pg 188)

Bluefish with Mustard Butter

Baked Spinach (Pg 91)

Carrot Cake (Pg 217)

Broiled Boston Schrod With Lemon Pecan Butter Sauce

Cooks Notes

Yield   4 Servings

Ingredients

4 - 10 oz	Fresh Boston Schrod Δ1 Fillets Δ2 ◊1
½ tsp	Paprika
½ tsp	Canola Oil
½ Cup	Lemon Butter Sauce (Pg 44)
2 Tbls	Pecan Pieces ◊2
2 Tbls	Fresh Parsley - chopped

Preparation

With Boston Schrod fillets, there are usually no bones to be concerned with; however, always take the time to inspect fillets to insure that they are boneless. Place the fillets on a broiling pan and sprinkle each fillet with paprika, then brush with oil place in the broiler, at least 3 inches from heat source, broil for 7 - 8 minutes, until done. Δ3 Add pecan pieces to Lemon Butter Sauce, mix well, to make a Lemon Pecan Butter Sauce. Remove fillets from broiler and place each on a dinner plate, top each with 2 Tbls Lemon Pecan Butter Sauce, sprinkle with chopped parsley, and serve.

HINTS

Δ1 Schrod is baby cod.

Δ2 The importance of quality fresh fish cannot be over emphasized. The difference between a superb fish dinner and an ordinary dinner begins with the quality and freshness of the fish.

Δ3 A properly cooked fillet of fresh Schrod will separate or 'flake'. To check for doneness, spread the 'flakes' apart and look into the center of the fish. The meat should be white in color, not transparent.

VARIATIONS

◊1 If fresh Boston Schrod is not available, several fresh lake and ocean fish are excellent broiled with this Lemon Pecan Butter Sauce, including Lake Trout, Pickerel, Walleye, Perch, Whitefish, Salmon, Sole, Monkfish and many others.

◊2 Omit the pecan pieces, if desired, to top fillets with Lemon Butter Sauce.

SUGGESTED WINES

dry, light to medium white:
L. Mawby Moira

OR

semi-dry, light to medium white:
Good Harbor Fishtown White

SUGGESTED DINNER MENU

Spanakopeta (Pg 76)

Caesar Salad (Pg 86)

Broiled Boston Schrod

Corn Casserole (Pg 193)

Strawberry Cheesecake (Pg 230)

PAN FRIED SKATE WINGS

YIELD   4 SERVINGS

INGREDIENTS

2 Lbs	Skate Wing Fillets △1 ◊1
2	Eggs
½ Cup	Water
¾ Cup	Herbal Breading (Pg 36) ◊2
½ Cup	Flour
½ Cup	Garlic Butter Sauce (Pg 45) ◊3
¼ Cup	Dry Red Wine
2 Tbls	Fresh Parsley - chopped

PREPARATION

With Skate Wing fillets, there are usually no bones to be concerned with; however, always take the time to inspect fillets to insure that they are boneless. In a small mixing bowl, mix egg and water together to make an egg wash. Place flour in a shallow pan and arrange fillets to the left of the flour, egg wash to the right. Place Herbal Breading in a shallow pan to the right of the egg wash. △2 Prepare fillets by dredging through flour, dusting off extra flour, then dipping in egg wash and placing in breading and coating both sides of fillet with breading. ◊4 As each fillet is breaded, place in the refrigerator to hold prior to cooking. Preheat sauté pan, add Garlic Butter Sauce, melt and get hot, without burning. Place fillets in hot butter, add sherry to pan (do not pour over fillets) and cook on each side until golden brown, about 4 minutes a side. To serve, divide fillets on 4 dinner plates, top with remaining sauce from pan and sprinkle with chopped parsley.

HINTS

Δ1 The importance of quality fresh fish cannot be over emphasized. The difference between a superb fish dinner and an ordinary dinner begins with the quality and freshness of the fish.

Δ2 When breading the fillets use a two handed method. One hand remains dry and the other hand is used to dip the fillets into the egg wash. By doing this you will not end up with a pound of breading stuck to your fingers.

VARIATIONS

◊1 The Skate Wing is the 'wing' of the Butterfly Ray and is moist and mild in flavor, resembling a scallop in flavor and texture. Skate wings may be hard to find; however, several fresh lake and ocean fish are excellent pan fried in this style, including Lake Trout, Perch, Whitefish, Halibut, Haddock, Sole, Schrod, Monkfish, and many others.

◊2 To lower the spice level in this dish, replace Herbal Breading with Almondine Breading (Pg 37).

◊3 Regular butter may be substituted for the Garlic Butter Sauce.

◊4 You may raise the spice level of this dish by adding Cajun Spice (Pg 50) after breading.

SUGGESTED WINES

semi-dry, light to medium white:
Leelanau Winter White

OR

dry, medium to heavy white:
Boskydel Soleil Blanc

SUGGESTED DINNER MENU

Crab Stuffed Mushrooms (Pg 73)

Inn Salad (Pg 87)

Pan Fried Skate Wings

Rice Pilaf (Pg 92)

Pecan Praline Cheesecake With Butterscotch Sauce (Pg 228)

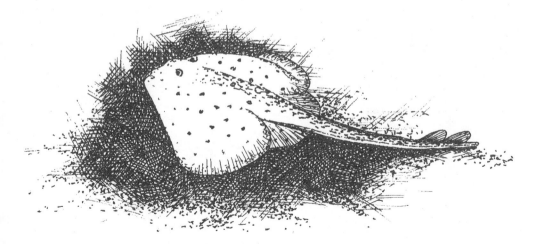

CREAMED FINNAN HADDIE

YIELD   4 SERVINGS

Cooks Notes

INGREDIENTS

1½ Lbs	Smoked Haddock Middles Δ1 ◊1
4 Cups	White Cream Sauce (Pg 51)
2 Tbls	Dry Sherry
2 Tbls	Fresh Lemon Juice
¼ Cup	Asiago Cheese - shredded ◊2
1 tsp	Paprika
2	Eggs - hard boiled and sliced
2 Tbls	Fresh Parsley - chopped

PREPARATION

Preheat oven to 375 degrees. If fillets are frozen, allow to thaw. Cut smoked fillets into ½ inch cubes and place in a casserole dish. Add sherry and lemon juice to White Cream Sauce Δ2, and pour over the fillets. Top fillets with shredded cheese then sprinkle on paprika and bake, uncovered, in oven at 375 degrees for 15 minutes, or until the casserole starts to bubble. Remove from oven, place sliced eggs on the top and sprinkle with chopped parsley to garnish.

HINTS

Δ1 Middles refers to the body of the fillet, not the tail end of the fillet.

Δ2 The White Cream Sauce must be warm in order for the sherry and lemon juice to mix well.

VARIATIONS

◊1 True Finnan Haddie starts with the finest Connolly Smoked Haddock. For this dish we don't recommend any substitute: this is by far John's personal favorite.

◊2 Any other hard cheese, such as Parmesan or Romano, may be substituted.

SUGGESTED WINES

dry, medium to heavy white:
L. Mawby Pinot Gris

OR

dry, light to medium red:
Leelanau Autumn Harvest

SUGGESTED DINNER MENU

Hummus (Pg 75)

Inn Salad (Pg 87)

Creamed Finnan Haddie

Rice Pilaf (Pg 92)

Chocolate Peanut Butter Ice Cream Pie (Pg 226)

SWORDFISH WITH LEMON BASIL BUTTER

YIELD   4 SERVINGS

INGREDIENTS

4 - 8 oz	Swordfish Steaks Δ1 ◊
¼ Cup	Canola Oil
½ Cup	Lemon Butter Sauce (Pg 44)
2 tsp	Fresh Basil Leaf - chopped
2 Tbls	Fresh Parsley - chopped

PREPARATION

Cooking will be done on an open flame char grill, pre-heated so that the rack is HOT. This will sear the steak so that the meat should not stick to the rack. Brush both sides of steaks with oil and lay on the grill rack. Cook on uncovered Δ2 grill 2 minutes then rotate fillet 90 degrees and cook another 2 mintues, then turn steak over, cook one minute, rotate 90 degrees, and cook another one minute. This procedure produces a nice 'checker board' of grill lines on the steak. After 6 minutes total cooking time Δ2, remove the fish from grill. Add chopped fresh basil to Lemon Butter Sauce. Place each steak on a dinner plate, top each with 2 Tbls Lemon Basil Butter, sprinkle with chopped parsley, and serve.

HINTS

Δ1 The importance of quality fresh fish cannot be over emphasized. The difference between a superb fish dinner and an ordinary dinner begins with the quality and freshness of the fish.

Δ2 Cooking on a covered grill will shorten cooking times given.

VARIATIONS

◊ The char grilling procedure can be used with any steak cut fish; or with firm fillet fish, such as Sturgeon, Whitefish, Halibut or Striped Bass. Some fillets of fish, like Sole and Schrod, are so tender that they break apart on the grill and should not be used. A rule of thumb is that if the fillet is solid and firm it should stand up to the grill.

SUGGESTED WINES

semi-dry, medium white:
Good Harbor Riesling

OR

dry, sparkling:
L. Mawby Blanc de Blancs

SUGGESTED DINNER MENU

Smoked Chub Paté (Pg 72)

Marinated Tomatoes (Pg 88)

Swordfish with Lemon Basil Butter

Gourmet Potatoes (Pg 194)

Pumpkin Walnut Cheesecake (Pg 218)

Baked Schrod Florentine

Yield   4 Servings

Cooks Notes

Ingredients

4 - 10 oz	Fresh Schrod Δ1 Fillets Δ2 ◊
1 Cup	Florentine Stuffing (Pg 40)
¼ tsp	Canola Oil
½ Cup	Lemon Butter Sauce (Pg 44)

Preparation

With Schrod fillets, there are usually no bones to be
concerned with; however, always take the time to inspect
fillets to insure that they are boneless. Preheat oven to 375
degrees. Place the fillets, skin side down, in a baking pan.
Brush tops of fillets with oil. Place ¼ cup Florentine
Stuffing on each fillet and shape it to the fillet covering
about ¾ of the fish. Place the stuffed Schrod in oven and
bake for 20 minutes. Remove from the oven and place
each fillet on a dinner plate, top each with 2 Tbls Lemon
Butter Sauce, and serve.

HINTS

Δ1 Schrod is baby cod.

Δ2 The importance of quality fresh fish cannot be over emphasized. The difference between a superb fish dinner and an ordinary dinner begins with the quality and freshness of the fish.

VARIATIONS

◊ If fresh Schrod is not available, several fresh lake and ocean fish are excellent baked in this manner, including Lake Trout, Pickerel, Walleye, Perch, Whitefish, Salmon, Sole, Lou de Mer and many others.

SUGGESTED WINES

semi-dry, light to medium white:
Leelanau Spring Splendor

OR

dry, medium white:
Good Harbor Chardonnay

SUGGESTED DINNER MENU

Pan Fried Alligator (Pg 71)

Caesar Salad (Pg 86)

Baked Schrod Florentine

Rice Pilaf (Pg 92)

White Chocolate Mousse (Pg 215)

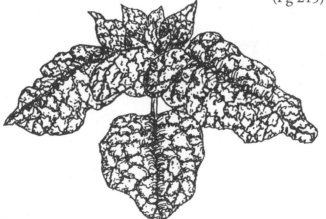

TOURNEDOS OF MONKFISH WITH PASTA

YIELD   4 SERVINGS

INGREDIENTS

4 - 6 oz	Fresh Monkfish Fillets Δ ◊1
¼ Cup	Flour
¼ Cup	Butter
1	Shallot - finely chopped ◊2
1 Cup	Dry White Table Wine
½ tsp	Whole Saffron
1	Bay Leaf
2 Cups	Heavy Cream
2 Cups	Egg Noodles - medium width
1 Large	Fresh Ripe Garden Tomato
1 Tbl	Fresh Parsley - chopped

PREPARATION

Blanch, skin, and dice tomato, and set aside. Cut Monkfish fillets into ½ inch thick medallions. Dust with flour and shake off excess. In a large sauté pan, melt half the butter and sauté the medallions for 3 - 4 minutes on each side, until done. Remove from pan and keep warm. Prepare egg noodles according to package directions, to yield 2 cups cooked, and set aside, keeping warm. In a saucepan, melt remaining butter and sauté finely chopped shallot until soft. Add wine and cook over low heat until liquid is reduced to half. Stir in half the saffron, the bay leaf, and cream. Cook the cream mixture over low heat, reducing it slowly until it is heavy enough to coat the fish. Strain the cream mixture and stir in the remaining saffron. Place the cooked, hot noodles on a serving platter. Arrange the medallions on the bed of noodles. Cover with the cream sauce and sprinkle diced tomato on top, then with chopped parsley and serve.

HINTS

Δ The importance of quality fresh fish cannot be over emphasized. The difference between a superb fish dinner and an ordinary dinner begins with the quality and freshness of the fish.

VARIATIONS

◊1 Monkfish, known also as Goosefish or Lotte, is sometimes referred to as the poor man's lobster. The fillet has the texture of lobster meat, is white in color and mild in flavor. If Monkfish is not available, Sea Scallops make an interesting substitute in this dish.

◊2 If shallots are not available, substitute 2 Tbls of finely chopped red onion.

SUGGESTED WINES

dry, medium to heavy white:
Boskydel Vignoles

OR

dry, medium to heavy red:
Good Harbor Coastal Red

SUGGESTED DINNER MENU

Cajun Shrimp (Pg 70)

Greek Salad (Pg 85)

Tournedos of Monkfish

Acorn Squash (Pg 90)

Peanut Butter Pie (Pg 216)

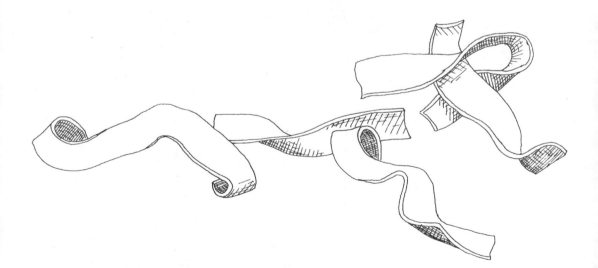

BARBECUED BLUEFISH WITH LEMON CAJUN BUTTER

YIELD   4 SERVINGS

INGREDIENTS

4 - 8 oz	Fresh Cape Bluefish Fillets Δ ◊1
2 Tbls	Olive Oil

Barbecue Spice

½ tsp	Salt
½ tsp	Black Pepper - ground
¼ tsp	Sugar
1 tsp	Garlic Puree
1 tsp	Onion - finely chopped
¼ tsp	Paprika
½ tsp	Cayenne Pepper

Lemon Cajun Butter

6 Tbls	Butter - softened
1 Medium	Shallot -finely chopped ◊2
½ tsp	Garlic Puree
1 tsp	Fresh Parsley - chopped
2 tsp	Lemon Juice

PREPARATION

Prepare barbecue spice mixture by combining in a small mixing bowl, salt, black pepper, sugar, garlic puree, chopped onion, paprika and cayenne pepper, mixing well. Brush both sides of each fillet with olive oil then sprinkle with Barbecue Spice to cover both sides. Let set, refrigerated, for 30 minutes.

Prepare Lemon Cajun Butter by combining in a mixing bowl, softened butter, chopped shallot, chopped parsley and lemon juice. Work together by hand until all liquid is absorbed by butter, then set in refrigerator to firm up. Cooking will be done on an open flame char grill, preheated so that the rack is HOT. This will sear the fillets so that the meat should not stick to the rack. After fillets have been coated with barbecue spice and rested for 30 minutes, place on the hot grill skin side down. Cook until the skin is crisp, about 7 minutes. Turn the fillets and cook an additional 2 - 3 minutes. Remove from grill and, put each fillet on a dinner plate, immediately place 2 Tbls Lemon Cajun Butter on each fillet and serve.

HINTS

Δ The importance of quality fresh fish cannot be over emphasized. The difference between a superb fish dinner and an ordinary dinner begins with the quality and freshness of the fish.

VARIATIONS

◊1 Cape Bluefish is one of the healthiest fish in the sea, it is high in Omega 3 oils, great for the heart. If Bluefish is not available the char grilling procedure can be used with any steak cut fish; or with firm fillet fish, such as Sturgeon, Whitefish, Halibut, Swordfish, Tuna, Mako Shark or Striped Bass. Some fillets of fish, like Sole and Schrod, are so tender that they break apart on the grill and should not be used. A rule of thumb is that if the fillet is solid and firm it should stand up to the grill.

◊2 If shallots are not available substitute 2 tsp finely chopped red onion.

SUGGESTED WINES

semi-dry, light white:
Good Harbor Trillium

OR

dry, medium to heavy white:
L. Mawby Vignoles

SUGGESTED DINNER MENU

Smoked Chub Paté (Pg 72)

Marinated Tomatoes (Pg 88)

Barbecued Bluefish

Gourmet Potatoes (Pg 194)

Creme Caramel (Pg 211)

NEW ENGLAND BOILED DINNER

YIELD   4 SERVINGS

INGREDIENTS

8 Cups	Water
¼ Lb	Bacon - thick sliced
3	Bay Leaves
3	Garlic Cloves
2 tsp	Thyme Leaf
¼ tsp	Crushed Red Pepper
2 Tbls	Kosher Salt
1 tsp	Black Peppercorns - whole
4 Medium	Carrots - peeled, diced 1 inch
8	New Potatoes - peeled, halved
6 Medium	White Onions - peeled
2	Turnips - peeled, halved ◊1
½ Head	White Cabbage - cut into four wedges
4 - 6 oz	Fresh Monkfish Fillets - halved Δ ◊2
2 Tbls	Fresh Parsley - chopped

PREPARATION

Prepare carrots, potatoes, onions, turnips, cabbage; and split fillets in half. In a large flat pot, bring water to a boil and add sliced bacon, bay leaves, garlic, thyme, crushed red pepper, salt and peppercorns. Reduce heat to a simmer and add carrots, potatoes, onions and turnips. Simmer for 15 - 20 minutes until carrots are tender. Do not overcook and soften vegetables. Add cabbage wedges and simmer for an aditional 5 minutes. Add fish fillets and simmer 6 minutes. Remove from the heat and allow to stand 4 minutes. Using a slotted spoon, carefully remove fish to the center of a large serving platter. Arrange all the vegetables and the bacon around the platter and spoon a little of the broth over everything. Sprinkle with chopped parsley and serve.

HINTS

Δ The importance of quality fresh fish cannot be over emphasized. The difference between a superb fish dinner and an ordinary dinner begins with the quality and freshness of the fish.

VARIATIONS

◊1 Rutabagas can be substituted for the turnips.
◊2 If fresh Monkfish is not available, Schrod or Haddock work well; or, for a heartier dish, Salmon or Cape Bluefish may be substituted.

SUGGESTED WINES

semi-dry, medium white:
Boskydel Seyval Blanc

OR

dry, medium to heavy red:
Leelanau Vis a Vis Red

SUGGESTED DINNER MENU

Hummus (Pg 75)

Inn Salad (Pg 87)

New England Boiled Dinner

Acorn Squash (Pg 90)

Chocolate Crepes with Kahlua Sauce (Pg 220)

SWORDFISH PICCATA

YIELD   4 SERVINGS

INGREDIENTS

8 - 3 oz	Fresh Swordfish Steaks - ¼ inch thick Δ ◊
¼ Cup	Flour
½ Cup	Butter
1 Tbl	Capers
2 Medium	Lemons - quartered
⅛ tsp	Salt
⅛ tsp	Black Pepper - ground
2 Tbls	Fresh Parsley - chopped

PREPARATION

Sprinkle Swordfish steaks with salt and pepper, let stand for 5 minutes. Dredge steaks through flour and remove any excess. In a sauté pan, melt half the butter and heat to a foam, without burning. Place Swordfish steaks into the pan and brown for 2 minutes on each side. In a separate sauté pan, melt remaining butter and heat to a foam, without burning. Add capers and lemon quarters, squeezing lemons as they are added, and sauté for 3 minutes, then remove the lemon quarters (and any seeds) and discard. Place the Swordfish into a serving dish and top with the caper butter sauce. Sprinkle top with chopped parsley and serve.

Hints

Δ The importance of quality fresh fish cannot be over emphasized. The difference between a superb fish dinner and an ordinary dinner begins with the quality and freshness of the fish.

Variations

◊ If fresh Swordfish is not available, Whitefish, Perch, Salmon, or Mako Shark may be substituted.

Suggested Wines

dry, medium to heavy white:
Leelanau Chardonnay

OR

semi-dry, light to medium white:
L. Mawby PGW Pun

Suggested Dinner Menu

Pan Fried Alligator (Pg 71)

Greek Salad (Pg 85)

Swordfish Piccata

Baked Spinach (Pg 91)

Heavenly Angel Pie (Pg 225)

HADDOCK FLORENTINE MORNAY

YIELD   4 SERVINGS

INGREDIENTS

4 - 8 oz	Fresh Haddock Fillets Δ ◊1
2 Cups	Water
2 Cups	White Table Wine
2	Bay Leaves
4 Sprigs	Fresh Parsley - stems and all
2 tsp	Salt
2 Cups	Florentine Stuffing (Pg 40)
2 Tbls	Fresh Parsley - chopped

Mornay Sauce

4 Cups	Half & Half
1 Lb	Swiss Cheese - shredded ◊2
½ tsp	Cayenne Pepper
2 tsp	White Pepper - ground
½ Cup	Flour
½ Cup	Butter

PREPARATION

In a sauté pan, heat to a near boil water, wine, bay leaves, parsley and salt, then add fillets and cover. Poach for 6 minutes, drain poaching liquid from pan, cover and keep fillets warm. While fillets are poaching, heat Florentine Stuffing in a saucepan, thoroughly. In a double boiler, make Mornay Sauce by heating half & half, cheese, cayenne pepper and white pepper, until cheese is thoroughly melted and mixed. In a sauce pan, make a roux by melting butter to a foam (do not burn) and stirring in flour. Cook roux over medium heat for 2 - 3 minutes, being careful not to burn. Add cheese sauce to the roux and mix well to complete the Mornay Sauce. On four individual dinner plates, divide hot Florentine Stuffing and place equal amounts into center of each plate, making a nest by creating a slight depression in the center of the stuffing with a large spoon. Remove fillets from sauté pan, and place into nests; then top each with Mornay Sauce, sprinkle with chopped parsley and serve.

HINTS

Δ The importance of quality fresh fish cannot be over emphasized. The difference between a superb fish dinner and an ordinary dinner begins with the quality and freshness of the fish.

VARIATIONS

◊1 If fresh Haddock is not available, several fresh lake and ocean fish are excellent poached in this recipe, including Lake Trout, Pickerel, Walleye, Perch, Whitefish, Salmon, Cape Bluefish, Schrod, Sole, Monkfish and many others.
◊2 Gruyere or any sharp white cheese may be substituted for Swiss.

SUGGESTED WINES

dry, sparkling:
L. Mawby Brut Cremant

OR

semi-dry, light to medium white:
Good Harbor Fishtown White

SUGGESTED DINNER MENU

Angels on Horseback (Pg 68)

Caesar Salad (Pg 86)

Haddock Florentine Mornay

Rice Pilaf (Pg 92)

Chocolate Filled Meringue Tarts (Pg 212)

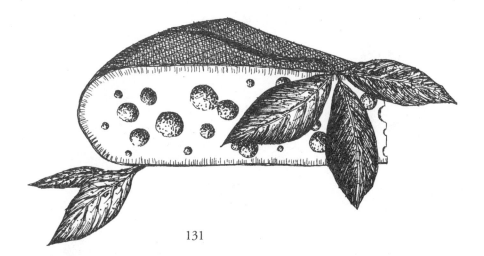

SAN FRANCISCO CIOPPINO

YIELD   4 SERVINGS

Cooks Notes

INGREDIENTS

1½ Lb	Fresh Assorted Fish Fillets - cubed Δ1 ◊
3 Cups	Marinara Sauce (Pg 57)
⅛ tsp	Worcestershire Sauce
8	Fresh Cherrystone Clams
8 Sprigs	Fresh Parsley - stems and all
4 Tbls	Garlic Butter Sauce (Pg 45)
8 Slices	Italian Bread - thickly sliced

PREPARATION

Cut fillets into 1 - 2 inch cubes. In a saucepan, heat Marinara sauce. Add cubed fillets and worcestershire sauce and bring just to a boil, taking care not to burn. Reduce heat and simmer for 20 minutes. In a separate saucepan place about ½ inch of water and the un-opened Δ2, fresh live clams. Cover and bring to a boil, cooking until clams open fully, about 10 minutes, being careful not to boil away all water. Spread Garlic Butter Sauce on Italian bread slices and broil until toasted. Divide fillets and Marinara sauce equally among four large soup bowls, place 2 Cherrystone clams, parsley sprigs, and one slice of toasted bread atop each. Serve with extra toasted bread on the side.

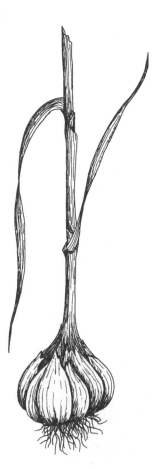

HINTS

Δ1 The importance of quality fresh fish cannot be over emphasized. The difference between a superb fish dinner and an ordinary dinner begins with the quality and freshness of the fish.

Δ2 If clams are not tightly shut, tap clam on countertop. If clam does not close, it is dead and should be discarded.

VARIATIONS

◊ The classic version of this dish requires a mixture of Schrod, Salmon, Cape Bluefish, and Haddock. Your choice of fish can vary: several fresh lake and ocean fish are excellent in this dish, including Lake Trout, Pickerel, Walleye, Whitefish, Monkfish, Swordfish, Tuna, Mako Shark and many others. Use as many varieties or as few as you desire.

SUGGESTED WINES

semi-dry, medium white:
Boskydel Seyval Blanc

OR

dry, medium to heavy red:
Good Harbor Coastal Red

SUGGESTED DINNER MENU

Pan Fried Alligator (Pg 71)

Greek Salad (Pg 85)

San Francisco Cioppino

Rice Pilaf (Pg 92)

Carrot Cake (Pg 217)

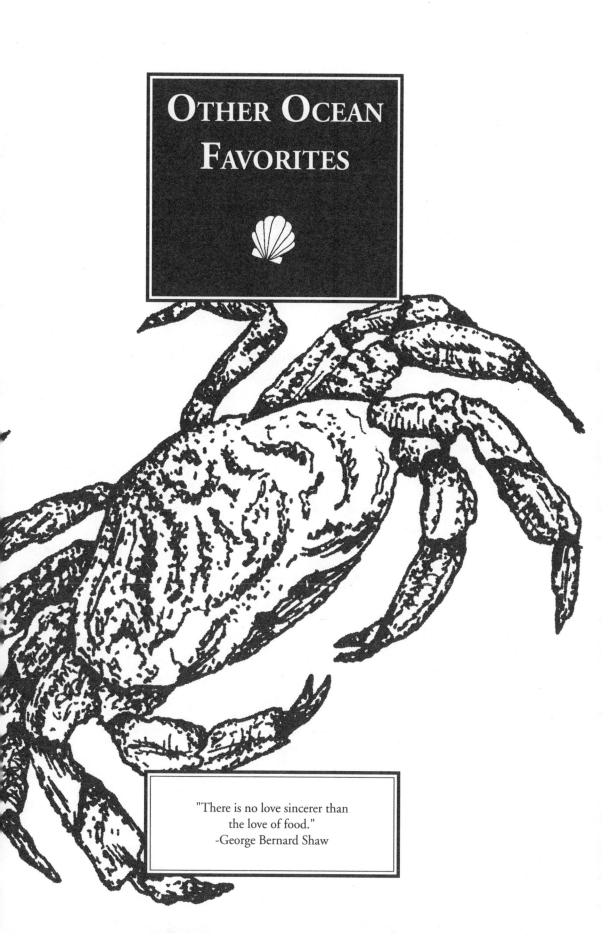

OTHER OCEAN FAVORITES

"There is no love sincerer than
the love of food."
-George Bernard Shaw

GULF SHRIMP FOUR SEASONS

YIELD   4 SERVINGS

Cooks Notes

INGREDIENTS

20	Jumbo Shrimp - shell on Δ1
1 tsp	Garlic Puree
1 Medium	Green Pepper - finely sliced
½ Medium	Onion - finely sliced
¼ Cup	Whole Button Mushrooms - sliced
¼ Cup	Pimentos - sliced
4 Tbls	Butter

PREPARATION

Remove shrimp from shell Δ2 and lay on side. Butterfly the shrimp by carefully inserting sharp knife into the large end of the shrimp, cutting in about ¾ of the way to the back, then cutting to the tail. Be careful not to cut through the shrimp. Rinse the shrimp clean, and lay open-faced on a broiling pan. In a sauté pan, melt 1 Tbl butter and sauté sliced pepper, sliced onion, sliced mushrooms and sliced pimentos for 6 - 8 minutes. In a small saucepan, melt 3 Tbls butter, add garlic puree and brush on the open faced shrimp. Then broil shrimp, no closer than 3 inches from heat, for 4 - 5 minutes, until slightly undercooked. Just before the shrimp are cooked, cover with the sautéed vegetables. Broil for one minute. Place in serving dish, carefully keeping vegetables atop the shrimp, and serve.

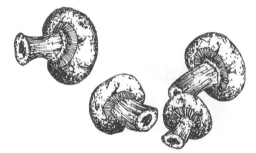

HINTS

Δ1 In the restaurant, we use what are called 21 x 25 Shrimp. This means 21 - 25 shrimp to the pound, and they are jumbo shrimp. Another common size is 15 x 20, a bit larger, and as good for this recipe. You may find IQF (Individually Quick Frozen) shrimp with the shell on. Do not buy cooked shrimp. If you find E-Z Peel shrimp, buy them - they have been cleaned and the shell will pull off easily, and are worth the extra cost.

Δ2 For the most professional looking dish, carefully leave tail on the shrimp when removing from the shell.

VARIATIONS

The choice of vegetables used may vary as tastes and availability dictate.

SUGGESTED WINES

dry, light to medium white:
Good Harbor Chardonnay

OR

semi-dry, medium white:
L. Mawby Sandpiper

SUGGESTED DINNER MENU

Cape Bluefish Chowder (Pg 84)

Caesar Salad (Pg 86)

Gulf Shrimp Four Seasons

Rice Pilaf (Pg 92)

Chocolate Crepes with Kahlua Sauce (Pg 220)

CRAB MEAT STUFFED SHRIMP

YIELD   4 SERVINGS

Cooks Notes

INGREDIENTS

20	Jumbo Shrimp - shell on Δ1
1¼ Cup	Crab Meat Stuffing (Pg 39)
3 Tbls	Parmesan Cheese - grated
1 Tbl	Paprika
½ Cup	Drawn Butter Δ2
2 Tbls	Fresh Parsley - chopped

PREPARATION

Remove shrimp from shell Δ3 and lay on side. Butterfly the shrimp by carefully inserting sharp knife into the large end of the shrimp, cutting in about ¾ of the way to the back, then cutting to the tail. Be careful not to cut through the shrimp. Rinse the shrimp clean and lay open faced in a shallow baking pan. Preheat oven to 350 degrees. Place 1 Tbl Crab Meat Stuffing on each shrimp and mold the stuffing to the shape of the shrimp. Sprinkle ½ tsp of grated Parmesan cheese and a titch of paprika on each shrimp. Seal each shrimp by pouring 1 tsp of drawn butter over each. Bake in preheated oven at 350 degrees for 15 minutes. To serve, divide equally on four dinner plates, sprinkling top of shrimp with chopped parsley. ◊

HINTS

Δ1 In the restaurant, we use what are called 21 x 25 Shrimp. This means 21 - 25 shrimp to the pound, and they are jumbo shrimp. Another common size is 15 x 20, a bit larger, and as good for this recipe. You may find IQF (Individually Quick Frozen) shrimp with the shell on. Do not buy cooked shrimp. If you find E-Z Peel shrimp, buy them - they have been cleaned and the shell will pull off easily, and are worth the extra cost.

Δ2 To make drawn butter, melt butter, allow solids to settle, and carefully pour off liquid. This liquid is drawn butter, and may be cooled and stored for later use. Plan to lose 25 - 35 percent of the beginning volume.

Δ3 For the most professional looking dish, carefully leave tail on the shrimp when removing from the shell.

VARIATIONS

◊ Topping the shrimp before serving with Lemon Butter Sauce (Pg 44) is a nice touch.

SUGGESTED WINES

dry, medium white:
Leelanau Vis a Vis White

OR

semi-dry, light to medium white:
Good Harbor Fishtown White

SUGGESTED DINNER MENU

Swiss Onion Soup (Pg 81)

Marinated Tomatoes (Pg 88)

Crab Meat Stuffed Shrimp

Gourmet Potatoes (Pg 194)

Strawberry Cheesecake (Pg 230)

SEAFOOD KABOB

YIELD   4 SERVINGS

INGREDIENTS

4	Jumbo Shrimp - shell on Δ1
½ Lb	Fresh Swordfish Steak ◊
½ Lb	Fresh Yellowfin Tuna Steak ◊
4 Large	Fresh Sea Scallops
1 Medium	Green Pepper - quartered
1 Medium	Red Onion - quartered
4 Large	Button Mushroom Caps
1 Tbl	Paprika
1½ Cups	Raspberry Viniagrette Dressing (Pg 60)
2 Cups	Rice Pilaf (Pg 92)

PREPARATION

Remove shrimp from shell and rinse. Cut each swordfish and tuna steak into four equal pieces. Split onion quarters by peeling layers apart to yield a total of eight pieces. Load skewers Δ2 by placing a piece of onion on the skewer, piercing outside of the onion first. Then skewer, in order, shrimp, Tuna, pepper quarter, Swordfish, mushroom cap, Sea Scallop and another onion section. Onion sections should curve around adjacent ingredients, holding them in place. Sprinkle kabobs with paprika. Lay skewered kabobs in a large casserole dish and pour 1 cup Raspberry Vinaigrette Dressing over kabobs. Marinate for at least 40 minutes, turning kabobs every 10 minutes to keep all sides moist. Prepare Rice Pilaf, allowing 25 minutes. In a small saucepan, heat remaining Raspberry Vinaigrette Dressing, stirring to keep well mixed. After marinating, discard marinade, and grill kabobs over a hot char grill, turning often, or broil in an oven, keeping kabobs at least 3 inches from heat. Cook for 12 minutes, turning one-quarter turn every three minutes. To serve, place ½ cup Rice Pilaf on each dinner plate, making an elongated nest; carefully remove cooked kabob ingredients, placing on Rice Pilaf nest in order, then pour over each 2 Tbls warmed, stirred, Raspberry Vinaigrette Dressing.

HINTS

Δ1 In the restaurant, we use what are called 21 x 25 Shrimp. This means 21 - 25 shrimp to the pound, and they are jumbo shrimp. Another common size is 15 x 20, a bit larger, and as good for this recipe. You may find IQF (Individually Quick Frozen) shrimp with the shell on. Do not buy cooked shrimp. If you find E-Z Peel shrimp, buy them - they have been cleaned and the shell will pull off easily, and are worth the extra cost.

Δ2 If you do not have metal skewers, bamboo skewers, available in most grocery stores, work well.

VARIATIONS

◊ Other firm fish may be substituted for the Swordfish or Tuna, such as Mako Shark or Monkfish.

SUGGESTED WINES

dry, light to medium white:
Boskydel Soleil Blanc

OR

semi-dry, light to medium red:
Good Harbor Harbor Red

SUGGESTED DINNER MENU

Angels on Horseback (Pg 68)

Inn Salad (Pg 87)

Seafood Kabob

Pumpkin Walnut Cheesecake (Pg 218)

PAN FRIED FROGLEGS ♣

YIELD   4 SERVINGS

Cooks Notes

INGREDIENTS

24	Froglegs Δ1
3 Cups	Milk
½ Cup	Flour
½ Cup	Garlic Butter Sauce (Pg 45)
¼ Cup	Dry Sherry
½ Cup	Lemon Butter Sauce (Pg 44)
2 Tbls	Fresh Parsley - chopped

PREPARATION

Thaw froglegs and rinse. In a small sealable container, place milk and layer froglegs into the milk so all of the legs are covered. Seal and refrigerate at least 24 hours Δ2. Drain milk and discard, leaving legs moist, then dredge through flour, shaking off unnecessary flour. In a large sauté pan, melt Garlic Butter Sauce, heating well without burning. Once a foam appears on the sauce, place froglegs in the sauce. Pour sherry in sauce, avoiding froglegs, and pan fry the legs over high heat for about 6 -7 minutes, turning often to avoid burning. Remove froglegs from sauté pan when done, place on serving platter, top with Lemon Butter Sauce, sprinkle with parsley and serve.

HINTS

Δ1 At the Inn, we use what are called 9 x 12 Froglegs. This size frogleg has 9 to 12 saddles (pair of legs) per pound. Do not use larger legs, as they may be less tender.

Δ2 The milk returns moisture to frozen froglegs prior to cooking. You may store legs in milk for 2 or 3 days (be sure to check the expiration date of the milk prior to usage so that it does not sour). This is a useful technique for frozen poultry and meat as well.

SUGGESTED WINES

semi-dry, medium white:
Good Harbor Riesling

OR

dry, rosé sparkling:
L. Mawby Brut Rosé

SUGGESTED DINNER MENU

Cajun Shrimp (Pg 70)

Caesar Salad (Pg 86)

Pan Fried Froglegs

Rice Pilaf (Pg 92)

White Chocolate Mousse (Pg 215)

STUFFED LOBSTER

YIELD   4 SERVINGS

INGREDIENTS

4 - 1 Lb	Live Lobsters
2 Cups	Crab Meat Stuffing (Pg 39)
½ Cup	Button Mushrooms - sliced
4 tsp	Parmesan Cheese - grated
1 tsp	Paprika
¾ Cup	Drawn Butter Δ1
1 Tbl	Canola Oil
4 Leaves	Lettuce
¼ Cup	Lemon Butter Sauce (Pg 44)
1 Tbl	Fresh Parsley - chopped

PREPARATION

Butterfly live lobsters by placing each on cutting board, legs down. Hold in place, and with a sharp knife, pierce through shell behind tentacles, pulling knife down and back through tail, taking care to not cut entirely through lobster. Then split the lobster body apart and remove the sack (located just behind the eyes). Rinse lobster with a solution of 1 cup cold water and 1 tsp salt. Δ2
Mix sliced mushrooms ◊ with Crab Meat Stuffing and place ¼ of the mixture in the cavity of each lobster. Sprinkle 1 tsp of Parmesan cheese on stuffing of each lobster, sprinkle stuffed lobster with paprika and top stuffing with 1 tsp drawn butter to seal the stuffing. Brush drawn butter on the tail meat, covering well; keep remaining butter warm, to serve with cooked lobster. Brush the exterior of the lobster shell with oil. Preheat oven to 375 degrees. Place lobsters on a baking sheet pan and cover the claws with a piece of lettuce. (The lettuce will protect the claw from exposure to intense heat and keep the meat inside moist.) Bake in oven at 375 degrees for 20 minutes. Remove from oven, place each lobster on a dinner plate, top stuffing of each lobster with 1 Tbl Lemon Butter Sauce, sprinkle with chopped parsley and serve with 2 Tbls drawn butter in dipping bowl on side.

HINTS

Δ1 To make drawn butter, melt butter, allow solids to settle, and carefully pour off liquid. This liquid is drawn butter, and may be cooled and stored for later use. Plan to lose 25 - 35 percent of the beginning volume.

Δ2 Some lobsters will contain a greenish substance, called tamale, which is edible, but may be rinsed out and discarded. Also, some lobsters will contain an egg mass, also edible, which may be left in place, cooked and eaten, or may be removed and discarded.

VARIATIONS

◊ The mushrooms are optional: though they help keep the stuffing moist during baking.

SUGGESTED WINES

dry, light to medium white:
Boskydel Vignoles

OR

semi-dry, light to medium white:
Good Harbor Trillium

SUGGESTED DINNER MENU

Parmesan Cheese Puffs
(Pg 78)

Inn Salad (Pg 87)

Stuffed Lobster

Stewed Tomatoes (Pg 89)

Pecan Praline Cheesecake
With Butterscotch Sauce
(Pg 228)

Clam Fritters

Yield   4 Servings

Cooks Notes

Ingredients

24	Live Cherrystone Clams Δ1 ◊
1 Cup	Pancake or Waffle Mix
½ Cup	Flour
2 tsp	Seafood Seasoning
1 tsp	Fresh Parsley - chopped
2	Eggs
1 Cup	Clam Juice Δ1
6 Drops	Tabasco Sauce
½ Cup	Dilled Tartar Sauce (Pg 53)

Preparation

Reserve juice Δ1, shuck and chop fresh clams. In a mixing bowl combine pancake mix, flour, seafood seasoning, chopped parsley flakes; mixing well. In a small bowl, beat eggs, 1 cup clam juice and Tabasco sauce. Stir egg mixture into flour mixture, then add chopped clams. Preheat non-stick griddle to 350 degrees (a non-stick sauté pan may be used, adjusting cooking time). On preheated griddle, drop batter by the Tbls, and cook for 2 - 3 minutes or until golden brown. Turn carefully and cook the other side another 2 - 3 minutes. Serve on platter, with Dilled Tartar Sauce in small serving bowl on side.

HINTS

Δ1 Reserve juice from clams during shucking, and strain. If necessary, bring up to 1 cup by adding purchased clam juice.

VARIATIONS

◊ If fresh clams are not available 2 - 16 oz cans of clams may be substituted; reserving 1 cup juice.

SUGGESTED WINES

dry, medium white:
Leelanau Chardonnay

OR

semi-dry, medium white:
Boskydel Seyval Blanc

SUGGESTED DINNER MENU

Smoked Chub Paté (Pg 72)

Inn Salad (Pg 87)

Clam Fritters

Rice Pilaf (Pg 92)

Chocolate Filled
Meringue Tarts (Pg 212)

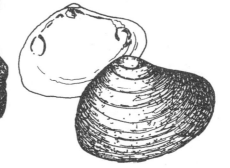

SCALLOPS & MUSSELS STEW

YIELD   6 SERVINGS

INGREDIENTS

2 Lbs	Nantucket Cape Scallops Δ1
30	Mussels - scrubbed and debearded Δ2
3 Tbls	Olive Oil
2 tsp	Garlic Puree
½ Cup	Onion - finely chopped
¼ Cup	Carrots - thinly julienned
1 Large	Fennel bulb - peeled and thinly julienned
2 Medium	Tomatoes - seeded, cut into ¼ inch strips
1 Tbl	Orange Peel - finely grated
½ tsp	Saffron
¼ Cup	White Table Wine
1¼ Cups	Clam Juice
4 Tbls	Garlic Butter Sauce (Pg 45)
8 Slices	Italian Bread

PREPARATION

Preheat oven to 350 degrees. Place scrubbed and debearded mussels and the scallops in a large glass casserole dish. In a sauté pan, heat olive oil, then add garlic puree, chopped onions, julienned carrots and julienned fennel. Cook for 5 minutes or until the vegetables begin to limp. Add tomato strips, grated orange peel, saffron, wine and clam juice and bring to a boil. Pour mixture into casserole over mussels and scallops and cover. Bake for 20 minutes or until the mussels have opened. Spread Garlic Butter Sauce on Italian bread slices and toast under broiler. Serve stew in six large soup bowls, using a slotted spoon to divide the scallops and mussels into the bowls, topping with the vegetables, then filling each bowl with the broth. Serve with toasted bread.

HINTS

Δ1 The scallops you choose make the dish. We recommend the finest scallop in the world, the Nantucket Cape Scallop, sometimes called Nantucket Bay Scallops. If the Nantucket is not available, other northern bay scallops are fine. Avoid southern scallops as their flavor leaves much to be desired.

Δ2 If mussels are not tightly shut, tap on countertop. If mussel does not close, it is dead and should be discarded. Scrub and debeard mussels immediately prior to use as the mussel when debearded will die. To debeard mussels run under cold water and remove the fiber mass protruding from the shell by pulling or cutting off. Scrub the shells clean to rid them of any barnacles or dirt.

SUGGESTED WINES

dry, medium white:
Leelanau Vis a Vis White

OR

dry, medium rosé:
Boskydel Rosé de Chaunac

SUGGESTED DINNER MENU

Hummus (Pg 75)

Greek Salad (Pg 85)

Scallops & Mussels Stew

Baked Spinach (Pg 91)

Lemon Bread (Pg 210)

CAPE SCALLOPS & SUN DRIED TOMATOES WITH PASTA

YIELD   4 SERVINGS

INGREDIENTS

1½ Lb	Nantucket Cape Scallops Δ1
3 Tbls	Olive Oil
2 Tbls	Garlic Puree
1 Cup	Sun Dried Tomatoes - julienned Δ2
½	Lemon - juice only
2 Tbls	Butter
2 Cups	Pasta ◊
3 Tbls	Fresh Parsley - chopped

PREPARATION

Prepare pasta according to package directions, to yield 2 cups, and keep warm. Drain scallops in colander. Heat a sauté pan to 'smoky hot', add oil, then add drained scallops. Immediately add garlic puree. After 30 seconds add julienned sun dried tomatoes and toss. Cook an additional 30 seconds and add lemon juice, butter and parsley. Remove from heat and toss or stir until the butter melts. Salt and pepper to taste. Serve immediately over cooked pasta, divided among four diner plates, and sprinkle with chopped parsley.

HINTS

Δ1 The scallops you choose make the dish. We recommend the finest scallop in the world, the Nantucket Cape Scallop, sometimes called Nantucket Bay Scallops. If the Nantucket is not available, other northern bay scallops are fine. Avoid southern scallops as their flavor leaves much to be desired.

Δ2 If the tomatoes are packed dry, steam or poach to soften before use; if packed in oil, drain and slice.

VARIATIONS

◊ Any style pasta noodle works with this recipe.

SUGGESTED WINES

dry, medium to heavy white:
Good Harbor Pinot Gris

OR

semi-dry, light to medium white:
L. Mawby PGW Pun

SUGGESTED DINNER MENU

Cajun Shrimp (Pg 70)

Inn Salad (Pg 87)

Cape Scallops & Sun Dried Tomatoes

Corn Casserole (Pg 193)

Chocolate Peanut Butter Ice Cream Pie (Pg 226)

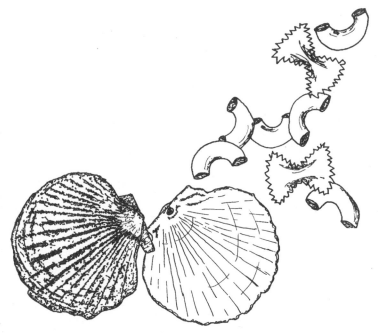

SEAFOOD ALFREDO

YIELD   4 SERVINGS

Cooks Notes

INGREDIENTS

4 Cups	Pasta Δ1
2 Cups	Heavy Cream
2 Cups	Half & Half
1 Lb	Baby Shrimp ◊
1 Lb	Nantucket Cape Scallops Δ2 ◊
½ Cup	Parmesan Cheese
2 Tbls	Black Peppercorns - crushed
4 Tbls	Fresh Parsley - chopped

PREPARATION

Prepare pasta according to package directions, drain, and keep warm. In a large sauté pan, combine heavy cream, half & half, shrimp and scallops. Heat to a boil. Cook the cream sauce for about 2 minuets at a boil, stirring to prevent scorching. Add Parmesan cheese and crushed peppercorns, stirring well. Allow sauce to cook to thicken for one minute. To serve, divide pasta evenly on four dinner plates, top with equal amounts of sauce, and sprinkle with chopped parsley.

HINTS

Δ1 Use linguini or fettucini with this recipe.

Δ2 The scallops you choose make the dish. We recommend the finest scallop in the world, the Nantucket Cape Scallop, sometimes called Nantucket Bay Scallops. If the Nantucket is not available, other northern bay scallops are fine. Avoid southern scallops as their flavor leaves much to be desired.

VARIATIONS

◊2 Other seafood may be substituted, for example, shelled Oysters, Monkfish medallions, shelled Mussels; or, a vegetarian Alfredo may be made by replacing the seafood with fresh peapods, broccoli, cauliflower, mushrooms, and tomatoes.

SUGGESTED WINES

dry, medium to heavy white:
L. Mawby Vignoles

OR

semi-dry, light to medium white:
Boskydel Seyval Blanc

SUGGESTED DINNER MENU

Pan Fried Alligator (Pg 71)

Inn Salad (Pg 87)

Seafood Alfredo

Lemon Bread (Pg 210)

SCANDINAVIAN SEAFOOD PASTA

YIELD   4 SERVINGS

Cooks Notes

INGREDIENTS

4 Cups	Swiss Onion Soup (Pg 81)
1 Lb	Nantucket Cape Scallops Δ1 ◊
1 Lb	Baby Shrimp ◊
4 Cups	Pasta Δ2
4 Tbls	Fresh Parsley - chopped

PREPARATION

Prepare pasta according to package directions, drain, and keep warm. In a large sauté pan, combine Swiss Onion Soup, shrimp and scallops. Heat to a boil. Cook the mixture for about 3 minutes at a boil, stirring to prevent scorching. To serve, divide pasta evenly on four dinner plates, top with equal amounts of sauce, and sprinkle with chopped parsley.

HINTS

Δ1 The scallops you choose make the dish. We recommend the finest scallop in the world, the Nantucket Cape Scallop, sometimes called Nantucket Bay Scallops. If the Nantucket is not available, other northern bay scallops are fine. Avoid southern scallops as their flavor leaves much to be desired.

Δ2 Use linguini or fettucini with this recipe.

VARIATIONS

◊ Other seafood may be substituted, for example, shelled Oysters, Monkfish medallions, shelled Mussels, etc. Or, a vegetarian pasta dish may be made by replacing the seafood with fresh peapods, broccoli, cauliflower, mushrooms, and tomatoes.

SUGGESTED WINES

dry, medium to heavy white:
Good Harbor Pinot Gris

OR

dry, light to medium red:
Leelanau Autumn Harvest

SUGGESTED DINNER MENU

Crab Stuffed Mushrooms (Pg 73)

Inn Salad (Pg 87)

Scandinavian Seafood Pasta

Creme Caramel (Pg 211)

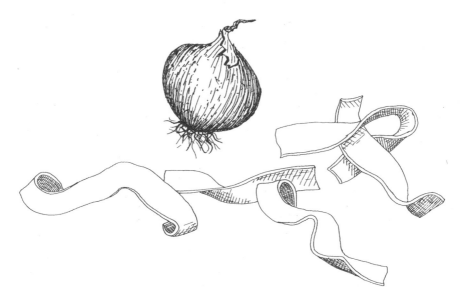

POULTRY & MEAT

"Satisfy your hearts with food and wine,
for therein is courage and strength."
-Homer

CHICKEN BREAST PARMESAN

YIELD   4 SERVINGS

INGREDIENTS

4 - 6 oz	Chicken Breasts - skinless and boneless ◊
1	Egg
1 Cup	Water
¼ Cup	Flour
1 Cup	Herbal Breading (Pg 36)
½ Cup	Canola Oil
2½ Cups	Marinara Sauce (Pg 57) Δ1
8 oz Pkg	Mozzarella Cheese Slices
4 Tbls	Parmesan Cheese - grated

PREPARATION

Make an egg wash by vigorously beating egg and water together in a small bowl. Dust each chicken breast in flour, dip in egg wash Δ2, then dredge through the Herbal Breading, making sure that all sides are covered. In a large sauté pan, add oil, heat sizzling hot without burning, add breaded chicken breasts and cook for 2 minutes, turn and cook on other side for an additional 2 minutes. Set breasts aside and cool Δ1. Preheat oven to 350 degrees. In a casserole large enough to lay the four chicken breasts side by side, place 1 cup Marinara Sauce and spread evenly. Sprinkle 2 Tbls grated Parmesan cheese over the Marinara Sauce. Place chicken breasts in casserole on top of sauce and top with remaining Marinara Sauce. Sprinkle remaining grated Parmesan over top of sauce. Cut cheese slices in half, and cover each chicken breast with 2 pieces of cheese. Bake in preheated oven at 350 degrees for 20 minutes.

HINTS

Δ1 The correct preparation of this dish depends on using either all cool or all hot ingredients. If the Marinara Sauce that will be added is freshly made and hot, do not cool fried chicken breasts, but assemble dish with warm chicken, and reduce baking time to 15 minutes. If you assemble dish with hot ingredients, do not cool before baking, as bacteria may grow in some parts of the casserole. If Marinara Sauce has been made ahead and is cool, follow preparation instructions.

Δ2 When breading the chicken breasts, use a two handed method. One hand remains dry and the other hand is used to dip the chicken into the egg wash. By doing this you will not end up with a pound of breading stuck to your fingers.

VARIATIONS

◊ Substitute veal for the chicken to make a nice veal parmesan.

SUGGESTED WINES

semi-dry, light to medium white:
Good Harbor Fishtown White

OR

dry, medium red:
Leelanau Autumn Harvest

SUGGESTED DINNER MENU

Angels on Horseback
(Pg 68)

Caesar Salad (Pg 86)

Chicken Breast Parmesan

Gourmet Potatoes (Pg 194)

Chocolate Raspberry
Brownies (Pg 224)

ORCHARD CHICKEN

YIELD   6 SERVINGS

INGREDIENTS

6 - 6 oz	Chicken Breasts - skinless & boneless ◊
2 tsp	Thyme Leaf
2 tsp	Poultry Seasoning
3 Cups	Apple Bread Stuffing (Pg 38)
1 Cups	Dried Cherry Glaze (Pg 43)
3 Cups	Rice Pilaf (Pg 92)
2 Tbls	Fresh Parsley - chopped

PREPARATION

With a tenderizing mallet, pound chicken breasts flat, using care to avoid tearing the meat. Preheat oven to 375 degrees. Prepare Rice Pilaf Δ. Lay each breast on a work surface with the inside of the breast facing up. Place ½ cup Apple Bread Stuffing in the center of each breast. Fold tail end of breast up and over the stuffing, fold each side of the breast up and over the stuffing, then invert the breast onto a baking pan. Sprinkle thyme and poultry seasoning on the top of the stuffed breasts. Bake chicken breasts and Rice Pilaf in preheated oven at 375 degrees for 20 minutes. In a small saucepan, warm Dried Cherry Glaze. Prepare each dinner plate by placing ½ cup of Rice Pilaf in the center of the plate, making a nest. Place stuffed breast in the nest and place 3 Tbls warmed Dried Cherry Glaze on each breast, then sprinkle with chopped parsley and serve.

HINTS

Δ Rice Pilaf may be prepared, but not baked, at this point. It may be cooked along with the chicken breasts, as the baking times and temperatures are nearly identical.

VARIATIONS

◊ Chicken breasts may be replaced with thick cut pork chops, with Apple Bread Stuffing placed in pockets cut into the chops.

SUGGESTED WINES

semi-dry, medium white:
L. Mawby Sandpiper

OR

dry, medium rosé:
Boskydel Rosé de Chaunac

SUGGESTED DINNER MENU

Sherry Butter Scallops
(Pg 69)

Inn Salad (Pg 87)

Orchard Chicken

Chocolate Crepes with
Kahlua Sauce (Pg 220)

CRAB MEAT STUFFED CHICKEN BREAST

YIELD   6 SERVINGS

INGREDIENTS

6 - 6 oz	Chicken Breasts - skinless & boneless ◊
2 tsp	Thyme Leaf
2 tsp	Poultry Seasoning
3 Cups	Crab Meat Stuffing (Pg 39)
¾ Cup	Lemon Butter Sauce (Pg 44)
¼ Cup	Pecan Pieces
3 Cups	Rice Pilaf (Pg 92)
2 Tbls	Fresh Parsley - chopped

PREPARATION

With a tenderizing mallet, pound chicken breasts flat, using care to avoid tearing the meat. Preheat oven to 375 degrees. Prepare Rice Pilaf Δ. Lay each breast on a work surface with the inside of the breast facing up. Place ½ cup Crab Meat Stuffing in the center of each breast. Fold tail end of breast up and over the stuffing, fold each side of the breast up and over the stuffing then invert the breast onto a baking pan. Sprinkle thyme and poultry seasoning on the top of the stuffed breasts. Bake chicken breasts and Rice Pilaf, in preheated oven at 375 degrees for 20 minutes. In a small saucepan, combine Lemon Butter Sauce and pecan pieces to make Lemon Pecan Butter Sauce. Prepare each dinner plate by placing ½ cup of Rice Pilaf in the center of the plate, making a nest. Place stuffed breast in the nest and place 3 Tbls Lemon Pecan Butter Sauce on each breast, then sprinkle with chopped parsley and serve.

HINTS

Δ Rice Pilaf may be prepared, but not baked, at this point. It may be cooked along with the chicken breasts, as the baking times and temperatures are nearly identical.

VARIATIONS

◊ Chicken breasts may be replaced with Schrod, Sole, or Whitefish. In the case of Schrod or Whitefish, a pocket may be cut into the fillet; with Sole, two fillets may be used as top and bottom with stuffing between.

SUGGESTED WINES

semi-dry, light to medium white:
Good Harbor Riesling

OR

dry, light to medium white:
L. Mawby Moira

SUGGESTED DINNER MENU

Swiss Onion Soup (Pg 81)

Greek Salad (Pg 85)

Crab Meat Stuffed Chicken Breast

White Chocolate Mousse (Pg 215)

Chicken Teriyaki

Yield   4 Servings

Cooks Notes

Ingredients

4 - 6 oz	Chicken Breasts - skinless & boneless ◊1
2 Cups	Teriyaki Sauce (Pg 49) Δ ◊2
¼ Cup	Fresh Green Peppers - ¼ inch cubes
¼ Cup	Fresh Zucchini - ¼ inch cubes
¼ Cup	Fresh Onion - ¼ inch cubes
¼ Cup	Fresh Button Mushrooms - sliced
1 Tbl	Canola Oil
2 Cups	Rice Pilaf (Pg 92)
2 Tbls	Fresh Parsley - chopped
½ Cup	Pungent Fruit Sauce (Pg 41)

Preparation

Place chicken breasts in shallow container, cover with
Teriyaki Sauce, refrigerate to marinate for 24 hours.
Prepare Rice Pilaf. Cooking will be done on an open
flame char grill, preheated so that the rack is HOT. This
will sear the chicken breast so that the meat should not
stick to the rack. Remove breasts from marinade, drain
well, and discard marinade. Place breasts on grill and cook
each side for 3 minutes, for a total cooking time of 6
minutes. During this grill time, in a sauté pan, heat oil to
'smoky hot', then add bell peppers, zucchini, onion and
mushrooms. Stirring and turning vegetables often, cook
for about 3 minutes (do not over cook vegetables, leaving
them hot but crunchy) ◊2. To serve, place on each dinner
plate ½ cup Rice Pilaf, beside that, a grilled chicken breast
and covering the final third of the plate, ½ cup vegetable
mixture. Sprinkle chopped parsley on the rice and serve
with 2 Tbls of Pungent Fruit Sauce in a small dipping
bowl on the side.

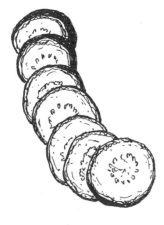

HINTS

Δ Teriyaki Sauce must be well chilled before using as marinade. If not made a day ahead of use, it should be well chilled for several hours before pouring over chicken breasts.

VARIATIONS

◊1 This recipe may be used with pork, veal, or beef or steak cuts of heartier fish such as Tuna, Swordfish or Mako Shark.

◊2 Teriyaki Sauce may be splashed on the vegetables when they are nearly cooked, using about 2 Tbls extra Teriyaki Sauce (do not save used marinade).

SUGGESTED WINES

semi-dry, light to medium white:
Leelanau Winter White

OR

dry, medium red:
Good Harbor Coastal Red

SUGGESTED DINNER MENU

Hummus (Pg 75)

Inn Salad (Pg 87)

Chicken Teriyaki

Carrot Cake (Pg 232)

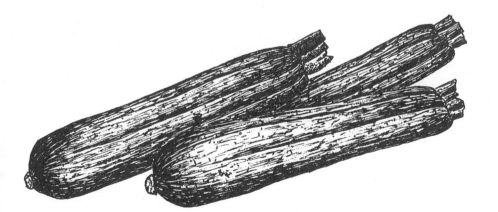

CHICKEN BREAST PICCATA

YIELD   4 SERVINGS

Cooks Notes

INGREDIENTS

4 - 6 oz	Chicken Breasts - skinless and boneless ◊
⅛ tsp	Salt
¼ tsp	Black Pepper - ground
¼ Cup	Flour
½ Cup	Butter
2 Tbls	Capers
3	Lemons - quartered
3 Tbls	Fresh Parsley - chopped

PREPARATION

With a tenderizing mallet, pound chicken breasts flat, using care to avoid tearing the meat. Season chicken breasts with salt and pepper, dredge through flour and remove any excess. In a sauté pan, melt ¼ cup butter and heat to a foam, without burning. Place chicken breasts in sauté pan and brown for 3 minutes each side, for a total cooking time of 6 minutes. In a separate sauté pan, melt remaining butter and heat to a foam, without burning. Add capers and lemon quarters, squeezing lemons as they are added, and sauté for 3 minutes, then remove the lemon quarters (and any seeds) and discard. Place chicken breasts in a serving dish and top with caper butter sauce, then sprinkle with chopped parsley and serve.

VARIATIONS

◊ Veal or pork tenderloin may be substituted for chicken breasts.

SUGGESTED WINES

dry, sparkling:
L. Mawby Blanc de Blancs

OR

dry, medium white:
Good Harbor Pinot Gris

SUGGESTED DINNER MENU

Crab Stuffed Mushrooms
(Pg 73)

Marinated Tomatoes
(Pg 88)

Chicken Breast Piccata

Corn Casserole (Pg 193)

Peanut Butter Pie (Pg 216)

CHICKEN WELLINGTON

YIELD   4 SERVINGS

INGREDIENTS

4 - 6 oz	Chicken Breasts - skinless and boneless
1¾ Cups	Dry White Table Wine
1 tsp	Basil Leaf
1 tsp	Rosemary
2 Tbls	Butter
½ Cup	Fresh Mushrooms - pureed
½ Cup	Celery - pureed
½ Cup	Onions - pureed
1 Box	Pepperidge Farm Puff Pastry Sheets Δ1
1	Egg
2 Tbls	Water
½ Cup	White Cream Sauce (Pg 51)
4 tsp	Fresh Parsley - chopped

PREPARATION

Make a marinade by mixing 1 cup wine, basil and rosemary; reserving 2 Tbls of marinade, place chicken breasts in shallow dish, add marinade and refrigerate for one hour. Δ2 Make a paté by pureeing mushrooms, celery and onion, adding 2 Tbls reserved marinade, and set aside under refrigeration. After breasts have marinated, heat ½ cup wine and butter in a sauté pan and sauté chicken breasts until they turn white, about 4 minutes. Set aside and cool.

 Cut each puff pastry sheet into four equal rectangles, making eight pieces. Place each breast on a piece of the pastry, top each breast with ¼ of the vegetable paté, then lay another pastry piece over breast and paté, pulling sides and ends to meet lower piece of pastry. Then, fold the lower piece of pastry over the top piece and pinch edges shut. Be sure that entire edge is sealed prior to cooking. In a small mixing bowl, make an egg wash by mixing egg and water together, then brush the top of the Wellington with egg wash. Preheat a convection oven Δ3 to 325 degrees, place Wellingtons on baking pan treated with non-stick spray, and cook for 20 minutes. Add remaining wine to White Cream Sauce Δ4, to make White Wine Cream Sauce. To serve, place each Wellington on a dinner plate, top each with 2 Tbls White Wine Cream Sauce and sprinkle with chopped parsley.

HINTS

Δ1 This puff pastry can be found at many food stores, in the freezer section. One box contains 2 sheets, each 14 inches by 11 inches.

Δ2 If marinade does not cover chicken, turn breasts in 30 minutes to marinate second side.

Δ3 This dish is best when cooked in a convection oven. If a convection oven is not available, cook in a preheated conventional oven at 375 degrees for 20 minutes. To achieve a golden brown color, it may be necessary to broil for 1 - 2 minutes.

Δ4 The White Cream Sauce must be warm in order for the wine to mix well.

SUGGESTED WINES

dry, medium to heavy white:
Good Harbor Vignoles

OR

dry, medium red:
Leelanau Vis a Vis Red

SUGGESTED DINNER MENU

Smoked Chub Paté (Pg 72)

Greek Salad (Pg 85)

Chicken Wellington

Baked Spinach (Pg 91)

Chocolate Raspberry Cheesecake (Pg 222)

Braised Lamb Shanks

Yield   4 Servings

Cooks Notes

Ingredients

8 Lbs	Lamb Shanks Δ1
½ Cup	Olive Oil
¼ Cup	Garlic Puree
2 tsp	Thyme Leaf
2 tsp	Whole Oregano
2 tsp	Basil Leaf
2 tsp	Rosemary
2 tsp	Ground Black Pepper - coarse
1 Large	Onion - sliced Δ2
4 Large	Tomatoes - poached and skinned
1 Cup	Water
2 Cups	Rice Pilaf (Pg 92)

Preparation

Mix olive oil and garlic puree together and rub over entire shank, to coat completely. Preheat oven to 350 degrees. Place shanks in a casserole dish. In a small mixing bowl, combine thyme, oregano, basil, rosemary and pepper to make seasoning mixture. Sprinkle seasoning over shanks and cover shanks with sliced onion. Bake shanks, uncovered, at 350 degrees for 20 minutes. Poach and skin tomatoes. Remove from oven and crush poached, skinned, tomatoes over the shanks with your hands and add water to casserole. Cover casserole and return to the oven. Reduce oven to 250 degrees and cook for 4 hours. Present shanks divided equally among four dinner plates, top shanks with tomato & onion, and serve with ½ cup of Rice Pilaf beside shanks.

HINTS

Δ1 Select the meatiest shanks available.

Δ2 Cut onion slices by first dividing onion in half from north pole to south pole, then cutting slices ⅛ - ¼ inch thick. This will yield more smaller slices, and better cover the lamb shanks.

SUGGESTED WINES

dry, light to medium red:
Boskydel DeChaunac

OR

semi-dry, medium white:
L. Mawby Sandpiper

SUGGESTED DINNER MENU

Cajun Shrimp (Pg 70)

Inn Salad (Pg 87)

Braised Lamb Shanks

Strawberry Cheesecake (Pg 230)

LINDA'S MEAT SAUCE & PASTA

YIELD   10 SERVINGS

INGREDIENTS

1½ Lbs	Ground Round
1 Cup	Onions - diced
3 - 29 oz Cans	Tomato Sauce - no salt added
6 oz Can	Tomato Paste - no salt added
8 oz Can	Diced Tomatoes
½ Cup	Sugar
1½ Tbls	Whole Oregano
1 Tbl	Basil Leaf
¼ tsp	Thyme Leaf
1 tsp	Black Pepper - ground
1½ tsp	Garlic Puree
3 Tbls	Fresh Parsley - chopped
2 Cups	Button Mushrooms - sliced
10 Cups	Pasta Δ1
½ Cup	Parmesan Cheese - grated Δ2

PREPARATION

In a sauté pan, brown ground round and diced onions together, mixing well and breaking up any large clumps of meat. Once fully browned, remove from heat and drain all excess liquid. In a large soup pot, combine and heat browned meat and onions, tomato sauce, tomato paste and diced tomatoes, mixing well. Add sugar, oregano, basil, thyme, pepper, garlic puree and parsley, mixing well. Bring to a boil, reduce heat and simmer for one hour, add mushrooms, and simmer for an additional 30 minutes. Carefully stir the mixture often during the cooking to prevent sticking.

Prepare pasta according to package directions, drain, and keep warm.

Serve meat sauce over pasta in a large pasta or soup bowl, sprinkle with grated Parmesan cheese.

HINTS

Δ1 Use linguini or fettucini with this recipe.
Δ2 Romano cheese may be substituted for the Parmesan.
Use freshly grated cheese whenever possible.

SUGGESTED WINES

dry, medium to heavy red:
Good Harbor Coastal Red

OR

dry, medium white:
Boskydel Soleil Blanc

SUGGESTED DINNER MENU

Crab Stuffed Mushrooms
(Pg 73)

Caesar Salad (Pg 86)

Linda's Meat Sauce & Pasta

Heavenly Angel Pie
(Pg 225)

PORK TENDERLOIN SAUTÉ

YIELD   6 SERVINGS

Cooks Notes

INGREDIENTS

2¼ Lbs	Pork Tenderloin Δ
¾ Cup	Flour
½ Cup	Garlic Butter Sauce (Pg 45)
½ Cup	Dry Sherry
3 Cups	Rice Pilaf (Pg 92)
1½ Cups	Mustard Sauce (Pg 48)
4 Tbls	Fresh Parsley -chopped

PREPARATION

Cut tenderloin into ½ inch thick medallions. Dust medallions with flour and shake off any excess. Prepare Rice Pilaf; and while rice is cooking, melt Garlic Butter Sauce in a large, preheated, sauté pan. In a small sauce pan, heat Mustard Sauce. When Garlic Butter Sauce is heated and starts to foam, add medallions. Then add sherry beside medallions and sauté for 8 minutes, turning medallions frequently to assure even cooking. Serve medallions in center of large dinner plates, with ½ cup Rice Pilaf on one side, and ¼ cup Mustard Sauce on the other side, and sprinkle entire plate with chopped parsley.

HINTS

Δ When purchasing tenderloin, make certain butcher trims the loin well, removing any silverskin and fat

SUGGESTED WINES

dry, light to medium red:
Leelanau Autumn Harvest

OR

dry, medium to heavy white:
L. Mawby Vignoles

SUGGESTED DINNER MENU

Crab Stuffed Mushrooms (Pg 73)

Caesar Salad (Pg 86)

Pork Tenderloin Sauté

Pecan Praline Cheesecake With Butterscotch Sauce (Pg 228)

PORK WELLINGTON

YIELD   4 SERVINGS

Cooks Notes

INGREDIENTS

4 - 6 oz	Pork Tenderloins
¼ Cup	Mushrooms - pureed
¼ Cup	Onions - pureed
¼ Cup	Ham - pureed
1 Tbl	Butter
½ tsp	Garlic Puree
1 Sheet	Pepperidge Farm Puff Pastry Sheets Δ1
1	Egg
2 Tbls	Water
1½ Cups	Mustard Sauce (Pg 48)
2 Cups	Rice Pilaf (Pg 92)
2 tsp	Fresh Parsley - chopped

PREPARATION

Make a paté by pureeing mushrooms, onions, and ham, adding garlic puree. In a sauté pan, melt butter and add paté, then simmer until liquid has been reduced by half. Set reduced paté aside to cool. Prepare Rice Pilaf.
Cut puff pastry sheet into four equal rectangles. Place each tenderloin on a piece of the pastry, pulling sides and ends up to meet each other and pinching edges shut. Be sure that entire edge is sealed prior to cooking. In a small mixing bowl, make an egg wash by mixing egg and water together, then brush the top of the Wellington with egg wash. Preheat a convection oven Δ2 to 325 degrees, place Wellingtons, seam side down, on baking pan treated with non-stick spray, and cook for 20 minutes. Warm Mustard Sauce. To serve, place each Wellington in the center of a dinner plate, add to each plate ½ cup Rice Pilaf on one side of Wellington, and ⅜ cup of Mustard Sauce on the other side of the Wellington, then sprinkle Rice Pilaf with chopped parsley.

HINTS

Δ1 This puff pastry can be found at many food stores, in the freezer section. One box contains 2 sheets, each 14 inches by 11 inches.

Δ2 This dish is best when cooked in a convection oven. If a convection oven is not available, cook in a preheated conventional oven at 375 degrees for 20 minutes. To achieve a golden brown color, it may be necessary to broil for 1 - 2 minutes.

SUGGESTED WINES

dry, light to medium red:
Boskydel DeChaunac

OR

semi-dry, light to medium white:
Good Harbor Trillium

SUGGESTED DINNER MENU

Hummus (Pg 75)

Inn Salad (Pg 87)

Pork Wellington

Chocolate Raspberry Cheesecake (Pg 222)

VEAL OSCAR

YIELD   4 SERVINGS

Cooks Notes

INGREDIENTS

1½ Lbs	Veal Leg Slices ◊
4 Tbls	Butter
12	Asparagus Spears- green, cooked
1 Cup	Hollandaise Sauce (Pg 55)
¼ Cup	Flour
¼ tsp	Paprika
1 Cup	Alaskan King Crab Meat
4 Tbls	Fresh Parsley - chopped

PREPARATION

With a tenderizing mallet, pound veal slices, using care to avoid tearing the meat. Blanch asparagus, and set aside. Prepare Hollandaise Sauce. In a preheated sauté pan, melt butter. In a small mixing bowl, mix ⅛ tsp paprika and flour, then dust veal slices with mixture, shaking off any excess. Sauté veal in pan for 30 seconds, turn and sauté for another 30 seconds, then turn the veal once more and add blanched asparagus and crab meat. Heat for one minute. In a serving dish, layer veal slices, top with crab meat, and then asparagus spears. Cover all with Hollandaise Sauce Δ, sprinkle with remaining paprika and chopped parsley, and serve immediately.

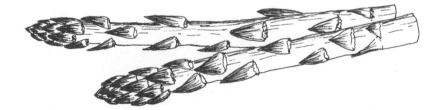

HINTS

Δ. At the Inn, we broil this dish, very briefly, at this point to brown the Hollandaise Sauce, omitting the paprika. This broiling must be done very rapidly under a very hot broiler to avoid breaking the sauce. We do not recommend that you try this method at home, but for the adventurous, we include it.

VARIATIONS

◊ Chicken breasts, pork tenderloin, or Whitefish, Schrod, Sole, and other fish fillets may be substituted for the veal.

SUGGESTED WINES

dry, medium to heavy white:
Leelanau Chardonnay

OR

dry, light rosé:
Boskydel Rosé de Chaunac

SUGGESTED DINNER MENU

Parmesan Cheese Puffs (Pg 78)

Inn Salad (Pg 87)

Veal Oscar

Rice Pilaf (Pg 92)

Peanut Butter Pie (Pg 216)

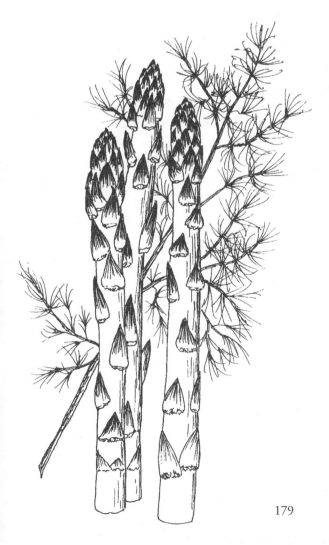

179

BRAISED BEEF SHORT RIBS

YIELD   4 SERVINGS

Cooks Notes

INGREDIENTS

4 Lbs	Beef Short Ribs Δ1
2 tsp	Thyme Leaf
2 tsp	Whole Oregano
2 tsp	Basil Leaf
2 tsp	Black Pepper - coarse ground
1 Large	Onion - sliced Δ2
4 Large	Tomatoes - poached and skinned
1 Cup	Water
2 Cups	Rice Pilaf (Pg 92)

PREPARATION

Preheat oven to 350 degrees. Place ribs in a casserole dish. In a small mixing bowl, combine thyme, oregano, basil and pepper to make seasoning mixture. Sprinkle seasoning over ribs and cover ribs with sliced onion. Bake ribs, uncovered, at 350 degrees for 20 minutes. Poach and skin tomatoes. Remove ribs from oven and crush poached, skinned, tomatoes over the ribs with your hands and add water to casserole. Cover casserole and return to the oven. Reduce oven to 250 degrees and cook for 4 hours. Present ribs divided equally among four dinner plates, top ribs with tomato & onion, and serve with ½ cup of Rice Pilaf beside ribs.

HINTS

Δ1 Select the meatiest ribs available.

Δ2 Cut onion slices by first dividing onion in half from north pole to south pole, then cutting slices ⅛ - ¼ inch thick. This will yield more, smaller slices, and better cover the short ribs.

SUGGESTED WINES

dry, medium to heavy red:
Good Harbor Coastal Red

OR

dry, medium to heavy white:
Leelanau Vis a Vis White

SUGGESTED DINNER MENU

Hummus (Pg 75)

Greek Salad (Pg 85)

Braised Beef Short Ribs

White Chocolate Mousse (Pg 215)

Beef Wellington

Yield   4 Servings

Ingredients

4 - 6 oz	Beef Tenderloins
¼ Cup	Mushrooms - pureed
¼ Cup	Onions - pureed
¼ Cup	Calves Liver - pureed
½ tsp	Garlic Puree
1 Tbl	Butter
2 Tbls	Canola Oil
1 Box	Pepperidge Farm Puff Pastry Sheets Δ1
1	Egg
2 Tbls	Water
½ Cup	Bearnaise Sauce (Pg 54)
2 tsp	Fresh Parsley - chopped

Preparation

Make a paté by pureeing mushrooms, onions, and calves liver, adding garlic puree. In a sauté pan, melt butter and add paté, then simmer until liquid has been reduced by half. Set reduced paté aside to cool.

In another sauté pan, place oil and get very hot. Place the tenderloins in pan and sear on all sides. This should only take a couple of minutes, as we are not cooking the tenderloin at this time, just searing in the juices. Set aside and let cool.

Cut each puff pastry sheet into four equal rectangles, making eight pieces. Place each tenderloin on a piece of the pastry, top each tenderloin with ¼ of the liver paté, then lay another pastry piece over tenderloin and paté, pulling sides and ends to meet lower piece of pastry. Then, fold the lower piece of pastry over the top piece and pinch edges shut. Be sure that entire edge is sealed prior to cooking. In a small mixing bowl, make an egg wash by mixing egg and water together, then brush the top of the Wellington with egg wash. Preheat a convection oven Δ2 to 325 degrees, place Wellingtons on baking pan treated with non-stick spray, and cook for 20 minutes. While cooking, prepare Bearnaise Sauce. To serve, place each Wellington on a dinner plate, top each with 2 Tbls Bearnaise Sauce and sprinkle with chopped parsley.

HINTS

Δ1 This puff pastry can be found at many food stores, in the freezer section. One box contains 2 sheets, each 14 inches by 11 inches.

Δ2 This dish is best when cooked in a convection oven. If a convection oven is not available, cook in a preheated conventional oven at 375 degrees for 20 minutes. To achieve a golden brown color, it may be necessary to broil for 1 - 2 minutes.

SUGGESTED WINES

dry, light to medium red:
Boskydel DeChaunac

OR

semi-dry, light to medium red:
Good Harbor Harbor Red

SUGGESTED DINNER MENU

Hummus (Pg 75)

Caesar Salad (Pg 86)

Beef Wellington

Acorn Squash (Pg 90)

Pumpkin Walnut Cheesecake (Pg 218)

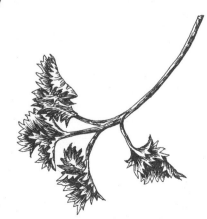

BRUNCH
FAVORITES

"Part of the secret of success in life
is to eat what you like and let
the food fight it out inside."
-Mark Twain

RED SKIN POTATO SALAD ♣

YIELD 1 GALLON

Cooks Notes

INGREDIENTS

4 Lbs	Small Red Skin Potatoes
2 Cups	Celery - chopped
1 Cup	Red Onion - finely chopped
2 Cups	Sour Cream
1 Cup	Mayonnaise
3 Tbls	Dill
½ tsp	White Pepper - ground
1 tsp	Salt

PREPARATION

In a soup pot, cover washed potatoes with water and boil until tender, about 20 minutes. Drain and while cooling: combine in a large mixing bowl, celery, red onion, sour cream, mayonnaise, dill, pepper and salt, mixing well. Chop the potatoes, leaving the skins on, into ¼ - ½ inch pieces and add to mixing bowl. Fold well to coat potatoes thoroughly. Store under refrigeration for at least 2 hours before serving.

Poppy Seed Pasta Salad ♣

Yield   14 Cups

Ingredients

1 Lb	Cooked Pasta ◊1
1 Medium	Red Onion - diced
2 Medium	Green Peppers - diced
2 Medium	Tomatoes - diced
1 Large	Cucumber - diced, skinless
1 Cup	Celery - diced
½ Lb	Pea Pods - fresh, blanched
2 Cups	Parmesan Cheese - grated
2 Tbls	Poppy Seeds
2 Cups	Greek Dressing (Pg 58)

Cooks Notes

Preparation

Prepare pasta according to package directions, drain, and rinse under cold running water. In a large mixing bowl, combine pasta with diced red onion, green pepper, tomato, cucumber, celery, blanched pea pods ◊2, Parmesan cheese, poppy seeds, and Greek Dressing. Mix well and chill before serving.

Hints

May be stored, sealed, under refrigeration for up to four days.

Variations

◊1 Shells, spirals, elbows - any short firm pasta shape works best.
◊2 These are the vegetables we use at the Inn; however, any fresh vegetables you like make for a great salad. Adding a drained can of dark red kidney beans is a nice touch.

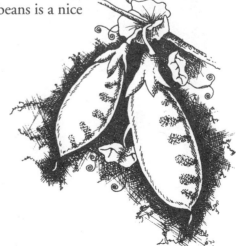

WILD RICE SALAD ♧

YIELD   12 CUPS

Cooks Notes

INGREDIENTS

2 - 6 oz Pkgs	Long Grain & Wild Rice Mix
15 oz Can	Sliced Water Chestnuts
2 - 6 oz Jars	Marinated Artichoke Hearts - halves
1 Cup	Celery - diced
2 Cups	Frozen Peas
2 Cups	Fresh Mushrooms - sliced
1½ Cups	Greek Dressing (Pg 58)

PREPARATION

Prepare rice according to package directions, set aside to chill, allowing one hour in refrigerator. Thaw peas. Drain water chestnuts and artichoke hearts. Clean and slice mushrooms, clean and dice celery. In a large mixing bowl, combine chilled rice, drained water chestnuts, drained artichoke heart halves, diced celery, peas, sliced mushrooms and Greek Dressing. Mix well and chill before serving.

CHILLED FRUIT SALAD ♣

YIELD **8 CUPS**

INGREDIENTS

Cooks Notes

3 Cups	Granny Smith Apples - diced ◊
2 Cups	Red Seedless Grapes - halved
½ Cup	Dried Tart Cherries
1½ Cups	Celery - chopped
2 Cups	Vanilla Yogurt - no-fat
½ Cup	Brown Sugar
1 Tbl	Vanilla Extract

PREPARATION

In a small mixing bowl, mix together yogurt, brown sugar, and vanilla extract and set aside Δ1. In a large mixing bowl, combine chopped celery, dried cherries, halved grapes and diced apples Δ2. Stir in yogurt sauce and chill well before serving.

Hints

Δ1 This sauce may be prepared a day ahead of time, and stored under refrigeration.

Δ2 Apples should be cut just before mixing to minimize browning; or spray with lemon juice ◊.

VARIATIONS

◊ Any tart, firm apple may be used. Cortland is a particularly useful apple in salads, as it will not discolor.

PEAS & PEANUTS ♣

YIELD 7 CUPS

Cooks Notes

INGREDIENTS

2 - 10oz Pkgs	Frozen Peas
3 Cups	Spanish Peanuts
1/4 Cup	Sugar
1/2 tsp	White Pepper - ground
1 Cup	Mayonnaise
1 Cup	Sour Cream

PREPARATION
Allow frozen peas to thaw overnight in refrigerator. In a mixing bowl, combine peas, peanuts, sugar, pepper, mayonnaise and sour cream, mixing well. Refrigerate for 4 to 6 hours prior to serving.

HINTS
May be stored, sealed, under refrigeration for up to five days.

MARINATED MUSHROOMS ♣

INGREDIENTS

Cooks Notes

1 Lb	Whole Button Mushrooms
1½ Cup	White Vinegar
¼ Cup	Canola Oil
1 Tbl	Water
1 Tbl	Salt
1 Tbl	Garlic Puree
¼ Cup	Onions - chopped
⅛ tsp	White Pepper - ground

PREPARATION

To make marinade, mix white vinegar, canola oil, water, salt and garlic puree; allow to sit unrefrigerated for 48 hours. In a small sauce pan, blanch mushrooms for 5 minutes, then drain. Mix onions, blanched mushrooms and pepper and add to the marinade. Allow to marinate, under refrigeration, for 24 hours before serving.

HINTS

May be stored under refrigeration no longer than seven days.

Hawaiian Beans ♣

Yield   10 Cups

Cooks Notes

Ingredients

15 oz Can	Dark Red Kidney Beans
15 oz Can	Butter Beans
15 oz Can	Garbanzo Beans (chick peas)
15 oz Can	Pineapple Chunks
1 Large	Onion - finely chopped
2 Medium	Green Peppers - finely chopped
2 - 15 oz Cans	Pork & Beans
1 Cup	Brown Sugar
3 Tbl	Molasses
1 Cup	Ketchup
5 Tbl	Worcestershire Sauce

Preparation

Open and drain well, kidney beans, butter beans, and garbanzo beans, and place in a large casserole. In a small mixing bowl, combine brown sugar, molasses, ketchup, worcestershire sauce, mixing well. To beans, add pineapple chunks and juice, chopped onions and green peppers, pork & beans, mix together and pour sauce from small mixing bowl over top. Bake covered at 350 degrees for one hour. Uncover and bake an additional 30 minutes.

Variations

Can be served hot or cold - and is best made a day in advance and well chilled if it is to be served cold

CORN CASSEROLE

YIELD   6 SERVINGS

INGREDIENTS

Cooks Notes

15½ oz Can	Whole Kernel Corn
15½ oz Can	Cream Style Corn
8½ oz Box	Jiffy Corn Muffin Mix
1 Cup	Sour Cream
¼ Lb	Butter

PREPARATION

Melt butter and add undrained whole kernel and cream
style corn, muffin mix and sour cream, mixing well. Pour
into a 1½ qt flat casserole. Bake at 350 degrees for 45
minutes, until top is brown and center is firm.

GOURMET POTATOES

YIELD   4 QUARTS

INGREDIENTS

5 Lbs	Potatoes - diced
1 Cup	Cream Cheese - softened
½ Cup	Melted Butter
½ Cup	Sour Cream
1 Small	Onion - grated
¼ Cup	Chives - chopped
¾ Cup	Sharp Cheddar Cheese - grated

PREPARATION

Scrub, peel, rinse and dice potatoes. In a large soup pot cook diced potatoes in water until very tender, about 15 - 20 minutes. Preheat oven to 350 degrees. Drain and place in a large mixing bowl. Mash potatoes and add softened cream cheese, melted butter, sour cream, grated onion and chopped chives, mixing well ◊. Place mixture in a large greased Δ casserole dish, and sprinkle grated cheese on top. Bake, uncovered, at 350 degrees for 20 minutes. Place under broiler for 1 - 2 minutes to brown top.

HINTS

Δ Spray non-stick coating works well here to keep potatoes from adhering to dish.

VARIATIONS

◊ Salt & Pepper to taste.

Main Street Chicken

Yield   8 Servings

Ingredients

2	Frying Chickens - cut up
4 oz	Jane's Krazy Mixed Up Salt Δ
1 Tbl	Black Pepper - coarse ground
3 Cups	Flour
4 tsp	Paprika
1 Cup	Olive Oil

Cooks Notes

Preparation

Cut any excess fat from frying chicken pieces, and wash chicken well. Very generously, sprinkle all sides of chicken pieces with Krazy Mixed Up Salt and pepper. Refrigerate chicken for 2 hours before continuing. Preheat oven to 350 degrees. In a shallow pan, mix flour and paprika and dredge each piece of chicken through the mixture. In a large sauté pan, place about an inch of olive oil and heat. Fry chicken pieces in oil, browning both sides of the chicken until golden brown. Drain and place browned chicken pieces in casserole dish, cover loosely with foil and bake at 350 degrees for 40 minutes, then uncover and bake another 20 minutes.

Hints

Δ Jane's Krazy Mixed Up Salt is a brand name salt and spice mixture available at most food stores. It is sold in 4 oz containers and for this recipe you will use nearly the entire container.

CHICKEN & ASPARAGUS CREPES

YIELD   18 SERVINGS

INGREDIENTS

Crepes

2	Eggs
1 Cup	Milk
1 Cup	Flour - sifted
¼ tsp	Salt
2 Tbls	Butter - melted

Filling

½ Lb	Asparagus Spears ◊1
2 Tbls	Shallots - finely chopped
6 Tbls	Butter
5 Tbls	Flour
1½ tsp	Wyler's Chicken Bouillon
1½ Cups	Water
½ Cup	Dry Sherry
1 Cup	Heavy Cream
1 tsp	Salt
1½ tsp	White Pepper - ground
2 Cups	Cooked Chicken Breasts - chopped ◊2
½ tsp	Thyme Leaf

PREPARATION

Prepare crepe batter by combining eggs, milk, sifted flour, salt and melted butter in a blender. Blend on medium speed for one minute or until batter is smooth. Then refrigerate batter at least one hour before cooking. Cook crepes in a crepe pan, or small, non-stick, sauté pan. Preheat pan until pan is hot, place 3 Tbls of crepe batter in center of pan, tilt pan to cover entire inner surface of pan with thin layer of batter. Cook crepe until firm and loose in pan. Cooked crepe should fall freely from pan when pan is inverted. In turn, cook additional crepes until all batter is used. When cooled, crepes can be stacked on wax or parchment paper.

Prepare crepe filling by cooking the asparagus until just tender, then cool and finely chop and set aside. In a sauté pan, melt butter and sauté shallots until soft, then stir in flour and cook for one minute. In a small mixing bowl,

combine chicken bouillon and water, mix well, then add to sauté pan slowly, stirring constantly until the sauce thickens and bubbles. Stir in sherry and simmer for 10 minutes. Add ½ cup heavy cream and salt & pepper, mix well. In a separate mixing bowl combine chopped chicken, chopped asparagus and thyme, mixing well. Then add 1½ cups cream sauce from sauté pan, mix well, and cool. Preheat oven to 350 degrees. Place ¼ cup mixture in the center of each crepe and roll crepe shut. Place filled crepes, seam down, side by side in a lightly greased baking dish. Whip remaining ½ cup heavy cream until stiff. Fold into remaining cream sauce and spoon over crepes. Bake at 350 degrees for 20 minutes or until bubbly hot.

VARIATIONS

◊1 Substitute one 10 oz package frozen asparagus spears if fresh asparagus is not available.

◊2 Ham may be substituted for chicken; if ham is used add 1 Tbl Dijon mustard to the sauce.

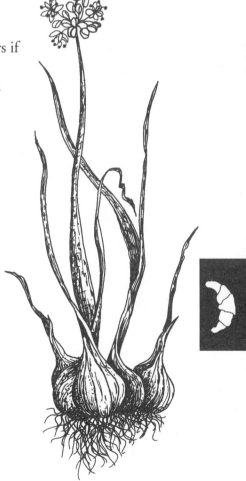

Chicken 'Pot' Pie

Yield   12 - 14 Servings

Cooks Notes

Ingredients

5⅓ Cups	Milk
1 Cup	Butter
⅔ Cup	Flour
2½ tsp	Wyler's Chicken Bouillon
2½ Cups	Water
2½ Cups	Onions - diced ¼ inch
2 ½ Cups	Celery - diced ¼ inch
2 ½ Cups	Carrots - diced ¼ inch
1 tsp	Thyme Leaf
1 tsp	White Pepper - ground
1 tsp	Salt
1 tsp	Poultry Seasoning
2½ Lbs	Chicken Meat - cubed ¼ inch Δ1 ◊1
1 Box	Pepperidge Farm Puff Pastry Sheets Δ2
1	Eggs
2 Tbls	Water

Preparation

Prepare a cream sauce by scalding milk in a small sauce pan. In a separate sauce pan make a roux by melting ⅔ cup butter, heating to a foam, without burning, then stirring in flour. Continue to stir and cook roux for 5 minutes over medium heat. Add scalded milk and stir until sauce is thick and of smooth consistency. Set aside. In a large soup pot mix water and chicken bouillon. Add ⅓ cup butter heating until butter is melted. Add diced onions, celery, carrots, thyme leaf, pepper, salt, and poultry seasoning; cover and cook for 15 minutes; being careful to leave the vegetables a little crisp. Preheat oven to 375 degrees. Add cooked cubed chicken meat and cream sauce; mixing well. Divide mixture between two 9 inch x 13 inch casserole dishes Δ3 ◊2. Cover each dish with a sheet of puff pastry. In a small mixing bowl, beat egg and 2 Tbls water together to make an egg wash. Brush top of pastry sheets. Bake for 20 minutes at 375 degrees or until the pastry browns.

Cooks Notes

HINTS

Δ1 Use leftover cooked chicken, or, if cooking the chicken for this recipe, place chicken in soup pot, cover with water, and add 2 bay leaves, some celery, onion, and carrots, then bring water to a boil, reduce heat and simmer breast meat for about 45 minutes, remove from water, chill and cube.

Δ2 This puff pastry can be found at many food stores, in the freezer section. One box contains 2 sheet, each 14 inches by 11 inches.

Δ3 At this point, mixture may be stored, sealed, under refrigeration for up to seven days before cooking and serving. If cooking after refrigerated storage, bake at 350 degrees for 45 minutes.

VARIATIONS

◊1 You may substitute cubed cooked beef or pork, replacing chicken bouillion with beef bouillon and omitting poultry seasoning.

◊2 You may make individual pot pies by using oven proof soup crocks, filling with the pot pie mixture, cutting puff pastry sheets to fit crock tops, and baking individually at 350 degrees for 20 minutes.

CHICKEN SOUFFLE ♣

YIELD   12 SERVINGS

INGREDIENTS

1 Loaf	Pepperidge Farm Original
3 Cups	Chicken Meat - cubed ¼ inch Δ ◊
1 Cup	Celery - finely chopped
½ Cup	Onions - finely chopped
½ Cup	Green Pepper - finely chopped
2 oz Jar	Pimento - finely chopped
½ Cup	Mayonnaise
5	Eggs - slightly beaten
3 Cups	Milk
1 Can	Cream of Mushroom Soup - condensed
½ Cup	Cheddar Cheese - grated
1 tsp	Paprika

PREPARATION

Trim the crusts from 6 slices of bread and cut bread into ¼ inch cubes. Place cubed bread in a 9 inch x 13 inch casserole. In a mixing bowl, combine cooked cubed chicken, chopped celery, onions, peppers, pimento and mayonnaise, mixing well, then layering over cubed bread in casserole. Trim crusts and cube remaining bread and layer over chicken mixture in casserole. In a mixing bowl, combine slightly beaten eggs and milk, stir and pour on top of casserole. Cover and refrigerate over night. Bake, uncovered, in a preheated oven at 325 degrees for 20 minutes. Spread condensed mushroom soup over top of casserole and bake another 45 minutes. Sprinkle grated cheese and paprika over the top and bake another 15 minutes, for a total cooking time of 80 minutes. Remove from the oven and allow to stand a few minutes before cutting portions.

Cooks Notes

HINTS

Δ Use leftover cooked chicken, or, if cooking the chicken for this recipe, place chicken in soup pot, cover with water, and add 2 bay leaves, some celery, onion, and carrots, then bring water to a boil, reduce heat and simmer breast meat for about 45 minutes, remove from water, chill and cube.

VARIATIONS

◊ Cooked, cubed turkey or ham may be substituted for chicken. If ham is used, add 3 Tbls Dijon Mustard to meat mixture.

SPINACH STUFFED SHELLS

YIELD   6 SERVINGS

INGREDIENTS

2 - 10 oz Pkgs	Frozen Spinach - chopped
2	Green Onions - finely chopped
1 Cup	Swiss Cheese - shredded
1 Cup	Ricotta Cheese
1 Cup	Romano Cheese - grated
1	Egg - lightly beaten
¼ tsp	Black Pepper - ground
⅛ tsp	Nutmeg - ground
8 oz	Jumbo Pasta Shells
3 Cups	Marinara Sauce (Pg 57)

PREPARATION

Squeeze spinach dry Δ1. In a large mixing bowl, prepare stuffing by combining chopped spinach, chopped green onions, Swiss and ricotta cheese, ½ cup Romano cheese, beaten egg, pepper, and nutmeg, mixing well. Prepare pasta shells according to package directions, being careful not to overcook, and draining and drying well before stuffing. Preheat oven to 375 degrees. Spread 1 cup Marinara Sauce over the bottom of a shallow 2 qt casserole dish. Stuff pasta shells with spinach mixture and set on top of sauce in casserole. Top stuffed shells with remaining sauce and sprinkle top with remaining Romano cheese Δ2. Bake, uncovered, at 375 degrees for 20 minutes or until heated through and bubbling.

HINTS

Δ1 It is important that the spinach be as dry as possible. To dry spinach, place the spinach in the center of a kitchen towel, bring up the sides and twist the cloth to squeeze out excess moisture.

Δ2 Stuffed shells may be covered and refrigerated for 24 hours should you desire to make them ahead.

SPINACH & BASIL QUICHE

YIELD   24 SERVINGS

INGREDIENTS

Cooks Notes

2 - 10 oz Pkgs	Frozen Spinach - finely chopped
1 Cup	Onion - diced
3	9 or 10 inch Pie Shells
1½ Cups	Swiss Cheese - shredded
1½ Cups	Sharp Cheddar Cheese - shredded
15	Eggs
4 Cups	Heavy Cream
1 Tbl	Basil Leaf
1 tsp	White Pepper - ground
½ tsp	Nutmeg - ground

PREPARATION

Squeeze spinach dry Δ. In a mixing bowl, combine spinach and diced onion, mix well and divide mixture among three pie shells. Preheat oven to 350 degrees. In a mixing bowl, combine shredded Swiss and cheddar cheeses, mix well. Evenly divide shredded cheeses and sprinkle over spinach and onion in shells. In a mixing bowl, combine eggs, cream, basil, pepper and nutmeg, mixing well. Pour mixture into shells over cheeses. Place shells on a sheet pan and bake at 350 degrees for one hour.

HINTS

Δ It is important that the spinach be as dry as possible. To dry spinach, place the spinach in the center of a kitchen towel, bring up the sides and twist the cloth to squeeze out excess moisture.

SEAFOOD QUICHE

YIELD   24 SERVINGS

INGREDIENTS

1 Lb	Alaskan King Crab Meat ◊
½ Lb	Nantucket Cape Scallops ◊
3	9 or 10 inch Pie Shells Δ
2½ Cups	Swiss Cheese - shredded
½ Cup	Smoked Cheddar Cheese - shredded
15	Eggs
4 Cups	Heavy Cream
1 Tbl	Basil Leaf
1 tsp	White Pepper - ground

PREPARATION

Preheat oven to 350 degrees. Mix crab meat and scallops together and divide evenly among the pie shells. In a mixing bowl, combine shredded Swiss and cheddar cheeses, mix well. Evenly divide shredded cheeses and sprinkle over seafood in shells. In a mixing bowl combine eggs, cream, basil and white pepper, mixing well. Pour mixture into shells over seafood and cheese. Place shells on a sheet pan and bake at 350 degrees for 50 minutes.

HINTS

Δ If using premade frozen shells, thaw shell completely before using.

VARIATIONS

◊1 The scallops you choose make the dish. We recommend the finest scallop in the world, the Nantucket Cape Scallop, sometimes called Nantucket Bay Scallops. If the Nantucket is not available, other northern bay scallops are fine. Avoid southern scallops as their flavor leaves much to be desired.

If desired, virtually any seafoods may be substituted for crab meat or scallops; for example, shrimp or poached fillets.

BARBECUE RIBS

YIELD   8 SERVINGS

INGREDIENTS

Cooks Notes

4 slabs	Pork Spare Ribs Δ1
6 Cups	Pineapple Juice
¾ Cup	Soy Sauce
1½ Cups	Barbecue Sauce (Pg 56)

PREPARATION

Trim ribs well and cut to desired size: it is best to have at least 2 bones per piece. In a small mixing bowl, combine pineapple juice and soy sauce, and mix well. Place rib pieces in a deep pan, pour pineapple juice and soy sauce over, cover with foil and bake at 325 degrees for 2 hours. Remove from oven Δ2. Generously brush on Barbecue Sauce and grill or bake at 325 degrees for 30 minutes.

HINTS

Δ1 At the Inn, we use what are called 1 and ¾ down ribs. These are small ribs, each slab weighing not more than 1 and ¾ pounds, and are the most tender ribs. Larger ribs tend to be less tender and require longer cooking time.
Δ2 At this point, ribs may be cooled and stored refrigerated. To finish preparation after storing, brush generously with Barbecue Sauce and grill or bake, allowing additional cooking time.

SAUSAGE & PEPPERS

YIELD   10 SERVINGS

INGREDIENTS

5 Lbs	Italian Sausage ◊
2	Bay Leaves
4 Tbls	Canola Oil
5 Large	Green Peppers - cubed ½ inch
3 Large	Onions - cubed ½ inch
2 Tbls	Basil Leaf
2 Tbls	Whole Oregano
1 Tbl	Thyme Leaf
2 - 29 oz Cans	Tomato Sauce - no salt added
1 - 29 oz Can	Chili Sauce

PREPARATION

In a large soup pot, add sausage and enough water to cover, then add bay leaves and bring to a boil. Cook sausage for 45 minutes, then remove from water, cool, and cut sausage into ½ inch medallions. In a large sauté pan, add oil and heat very hot, without burning. Add sausage, cubed peppers, cubed onions, basil, oregano, and thyme and sauté until the vegetables become limp. Add tomato and chili sauces and simmer for 30 minutes. Δ

HINTS

Δ This is best served over rice or noodles.

VARIATIONS

◊ Other sausages, including bratwurst, Polish, smoked, or choriso may be substituted for Italian sausage, or used in combination.

PEPPER STEAK

YIELD   8 SERVINGS

INGREDIENTS   *Cooks Notes*

3 Lbs	Beef Tenderloin Tips ◊
⅓ Cup	Canola Oil
1¼ tsp	Wyler's Beef Bouillon
1½ Cups	Water
1¼ tsp	Salt
¼ tsp	Black Pepper - ground
½ Cup	Onion - finely chopped
1 tsp	Garlic Puree
2 Large	Green Peppers - julienned
1 Lb	Whole Button Mushrooms
⅓ Cup	Cornstarch
1 Tbl	Light Soy Sauce
4 Large	Tomatoes - quartered

PREPARATION

Slice tenderloin tips into thin strips. In a large sauté pan heat oil and brown tenderloin strips. In a small mixing bowl, combine beef bouillion and 1¼ cups water, mix well and add to sauté pan; then add to sauté pan, salt, pepper, chopped onion, and garlic puree, mixing well. Cover and simmer for 20 minutes, then add julienned peppers and whole mushrooms. Cover and simmer until vegetable are tender crisp, about four minutes. In a samll mixing bowl, combine cornstarch and water Δ1, then add soy sauce, stir well and pour mixture into sauté pan. Cook, stirring until sauce is thickened. Add quartered tomatoes and cook uncovered for three minutes. Δ2

HINTS

Δ1 To improve mixing, add cold water to corn starch, rather than corn starch to water.
Δ2 This is best served over rice or noodles.

VARIATIONS

◊ Stewing meat may be substituted, however, plan on an additional 15 - 20 minutes cooking time.

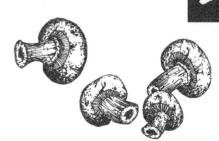

Country Inn Ham & Glaze

Yield   24 Servings

Cooks Notes

Ingredients

14 Lb	Uncooked Smoked Banjo Ham
1 Cup	Brown Sugar
½ Cup	Dry Sherry
¼ Cup	Honey
¼ Cup	Dijon Mustard

Preparation

Preheat oven to 300 degrees. Place ham in a large baking pan, cover with foil and bake at 300 degrees for one hour. In a small mixing bowl, combine brown sugar, sherry, honey and mustard, mixing well. Remove ham from oven, remove foil and score ham, making cuts ⅛ inch deep about an inch apart. Generously glaze ham with mixture. Return to oven, uncovered, to bake for an additional two hours at 300 degrees, glazing ham every 20 minutes during that two hours cooking time. Cool ham well before carving.

PERFECT ENDINGS

"After delicious fare
I take no common food."
-Petronius

LEMON BREAD

YIELD   3 LOAVES

INGREDIENTS

4½ Cups	Sugar
1½ Cups	Butter - softened
6	Eggs
4½ Cups	Flour - sifted
½ tsp	Baking Soda
½ tsp	Salt
1½ Cups	Buttermilk
4	Lemons

PREPARATION

Preheat oven to 325 degrees. In a mixing bowl, combine 3 cups sugar and softened butter, mix well. Add eggs, one egg at a time then add sifted flour, baking soda, salt and buttermilk, mix well. Grate 2 lemons for zest, add zest to mixing bowl, mix thoroughly. Divide batter into three greased bread pans and bake for one hour at 325 degrees. Remove from oven and cool for five minutes. While loaves are cooling, in a sauce pan over low heat, mix together juice of all four lemons and 1½ cups sugar. Remove loaves from pans and, with a table fork, poke a few holes in the top of the bread. After lemon juice and sugar mixture is well mixed and warm, brush mixture on top of the loaves of lemon bread.

VARIATIONS

Orange zest and juice may be substituted for lemon to make orange bread.

CREME CARAMEL

YIELD   6 SERVINGS

INGREDIENTS   *Cooks Notes*

Caramel
¾ Cup   Sugar
1 Tbl   Water

Custard
2 Cups   Half & Half
½ Cup   Sugar
⅛ tsp   Salt
1 tsp   Vanilla
3   Eggs

Whipped Cream
¾ Cup   Heavy Cream
½ tsp   Vanilla
1 tsp   Powdered Sugar

PREPARATION

Preheat oven to 350 degrees. Place small mixing bowl in
freezer for making whipped cream. To make caramel, in a
sauce pan, over low heat mix sugar and water and cara-
melize until a golden brown. Quickly pour 2 Tbls in the
bottom of each of 6 custard dishes or soup cups.
In a mixing bowl, combine half & half, sugar, salt, vanilla
and eggs and beat well until thoroughly mixed. Divide
custard into custard dishes, atop caramel. Line the bottom
of a deep pan with a few sheets of newspaper. The newspaper will keep the water from coming to a boil and
cooking the custard too rapidly. Place filled custard dishes
on the paper and fill the pan ¾ of the way up the custard
dishes with water. Place in oven at 350 degrees and cook
for an hour or until done, testing for doneness by probing
custard with a toothpick. Custard is done when toothpick
comes out clean. Store the Creme Caramel, refrigerated,
in custard dishes until ready to serve. Prepare whipped
cream by placing heavy cream, vanilla and powdered sugar
in small mixing bowl chilled in freezer, whip until stiff
peak. Then invert each custard cup onto a dessert plate,
add a dollop of whipped cream beside the Creme Caramel
and serve.

211

Chocolate Filled Meringue Tarts

Yield   48 Mini Tarts

Ingredients

Meringues

4	Egg Whites
1 Cup	Sugar
¼ tsp	Cream of Tartar

Chocolate Filling

6	Eggs
5 Tbls	Sugar
2 Cups	Semisweet Chocolate Morsels
½ Cup	Butter - softened
1 Cup	Heavy Cream

Preparation

Preheat oven to 200 degrees. Make meringue batter by beating egg whites until stiff, not dry, then adding sugar and cream of tartar to the mixture slowly, beating well. Put a rounded tsp of meringue batter in each cavity of a mini tart pan Δ. When all cavities are filled, use a rounded spoon to hollow out each meringue. Bake at 200 degrees for one hour. Turn off oven, open oven door slightly and allow meringues to cool for one hour before removing from oven Δ2. While meringues are baking, make chocolate filling by combining in a double boiler over low heat, eggs, sugar, semi-sweet chocolate morsels, softened butter and heavy cream, mixing well until smooth. Cook until thick, then set aside to cool. To serve, fill meringue shells with chilled chocolate filling and serve immediately, do not store filled meringues.

Cooks Notes

HINTS

Δ At the Inn we use pans with cavities of about 1½ inch diameter. If you wish, you may make larger meringues, by using cup cake pans with more batter per cavity.

Δ2 Meringues may be stored, sealed, before use for up to two weeks. Do not refrigerate, as meringues will absorb moisture and spoil.

VARIATIONS

Meringues may be filled with many other things, including fruit pie fillings. At the Inn, we also use lemon cream.

CHEESE WOOKIES

YIELD   150 WOOKIES

Cooks Notes

INGREDIENTS

½ Lb	Butter - softened
½ Lb	Margarine - softened
1 Lb	Sharp Cheddar Cheese - shredded
4 Cups	Flour
	Salt

PREPARATION
In a mixing bowl, combine softened butter, softened margarine, shredded cheese and flour, mixing well. Refrigerate dough for one hour. Roll dough into round balls the diameter of a nickel. Place on a cookie sheet pan and bake at 325 degrees for 25 minutes. Remove from oven, place wookies on brown paper on countertop and very lightly salt. Allow to cool and serve.

HINTS
May be stored, sealed, under refrigeration for up to two weeks.

VARIATIONS
Grandma's original recipe called for almond slices and egg whites. To try the original version, slightly flatten wookies with thumb before baking, place almond slice on flattened wookie top, brush top with beaten egg white, then bake and finish as above.

WHITE CHOCOLATE MOUSSE

YIELD   16 SERVINGS

INGREDIENTS   *Cooks Notes*

2¼ Cups	Heavy Cream
1 Env	Knox Unflavored Gelatin
18 oz	White Chocolate Brick
½ tsp	Vanilla
2	Egg Whites
¼ tsp	Salt
2 Tbls	Sugar
6 oz	IQF Raspberries
1½ Cups	Sugar

PREPARATION

In a saucepan, place 1¼ cups heavy cream, sprinkle gelatin on top and let stand 5 minutes. Break chocolate brick into pieces, add to saucepan, cooking over low heat until melted and mixture is smooth. Transfer mixture to a mixing bowl and chill for ten minutes. In another mixing bowl combine remaining heavy cream and vanilla, whipping to a peak. In still another mixing bowl combine egg whites and salt and beat to a peak. Gradually add 2 Tbls sugar until a stiff peak forms. To the chilled chocolate, fold in whipped cream and egg whites. to make mousse. Divide mousse, placing ½ cup mousse in each of 16 wine glasses and chill a minimum of three hours. While mousse is chilling, mix, in a food processor, thawed raspberries and 1½ cups sugar, then chill well. To serve mousse, top each glass with 2 Tbls raspberry sauce and garnish with a fresh mint leaf.

PEANUT BUTTER PIE ♣

YIELD   ONE PIE

Cooks Notes

INGREDIENTS

Crust
¼ Cup	Butter - softened
¼ Cup	Sugar
1 Cup	Graham Cracker Crumbs

Filling
1 Cup	Cream Cheese - softened
1 Cup	Creamy Peanut Butter
2 Tbls	Butter - softened
1 Cup	Powdered Sugar
2 Tbls	Powdered Sugar
½ Cup	Heavy Cream
1 Tbl	Vanilla Extract

Topping
½ Cup	Heavy Cream
1 Cup	Semisweet Chocolate Morsels

PREPARATION

To make crust, in a mixing bowl, combine graham cracker crumbs, sugar and softened butter. Mix together and press into a buttered 9 inch pie pan, form shell and refrigerate one hour.

To make filling, in a mixing bowl, with an electric mixer, combine and mix well softened cream cheese, softened butter and peanut butter. Add 1 cup powdered sugar and beat until fluffy. In another mixing bowl, beat heavy cream until a peak forms. Gradually add 2 Tbls powdered sugar and vanilla and beat to a stiff peak. Combine beaten cream with the peanut butter mixture, mixing well. Place filling in shell and refrigerate till firm, 2 - 3 hours.

To make topping, bring heavy cream to a simmer in a small saucepan over low heat. Add chocolate and stir till melted and smooth. Cool to lukewarm. After filling has firmed for 2 - 3 hours, spread topping over pie. Refrigerate again until topping is firm, about 3 hours. Cut into eight pieces, and serve.

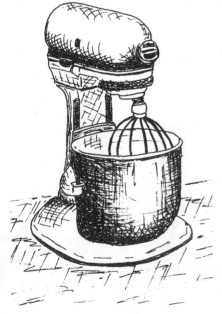

Carrot Cake

YIELD   ONE CAKE

INGREDIENTS   *Cooks Notes*

2 Cups	Flour
2 tsp	Baking Soda
1 tsp	Salt
1¼ Cups	Canola Oil
4	Eggs - beaten
3½ Cups	Carrots - grated
2 Cups	Sugar - granulated
1 tsp	Vanilla
2 tsp	Cinnamon - ground
8 oz	Cream Cheese - softened
1½ Sticks	Margarine - softened
2 Cups	Powdered Sugar
½ Cup	Coconut - shredded
½ Cup	Walnuts - chopped

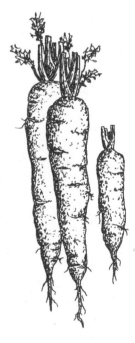

Preparation

Preheat oven to 350 degrees. Prepare batter by combining, in a mixing bowl, flour, baking soda and salt, mixing well. Add oil and mix well. Add beaten eggs, grated carrots, granulated sugar, vanilla and cinnamon, mixing well. Pour batter into two 8 inch cake rounds and bake for 35 - 45 minutes at 350 degrees. Cake is done when a probe into the center of the cake comes out clean.

Prepare icing by combining in a mixing bowl, softened cream cheese and softened margarine, mixing well. Add powdered sugar, mixing well. Then add shredded coconut and chopped walnuts, mixing well.

After baked cake is cool, spread the icing on the top of one of the cakes, then place the other cake on top and cover the entire cake, sides and top. Refrigerate prior to service, at least one hour.

Hints

This cake will stay moist for several days if stored, sealed, under refrigeration.

PUMPKIN WALNUT CHEESECAKE ♣

YIELD   ONE CHEESECAKE

Cooks Notes

INGREDIENTS

Crust
1 Cup	Flour
2 Cups	Powdered Sugar
¾ Cup	Butter - melted
1 Cup.	Walnuts - chopped
1½ tsp	Vanilla
1	Egg Yolk

Filling
2 Lbs	Cream Cheese - softened
2 Cups	Sugar
3	Eggs
1	Egg yolk
1½ Cups	Pumpkin Pie Filling
1 Tbl	Cinnamon - ground
½ tsp	Nutmeg - ground
3 Tbls	Flour

Topping
½ Cup	Brown Sugar
⅓ Cup	Flour
¼ Cup	Butter- softened

Cooks Notes

Preparation

Prepare crust by combining in a mixing bowl, flour, sugar, melted butter, chopped walnuts, vanilla, and egg yolk, mixing well with hands. Place in 9½ inch spring form pan, covering bottom and come up sides ¼ inch. Preheat oven to 375 degrees.

Prepare filling by beating in a mixing bowl softened cream cheese until fluffy. Add sugar slowly, blending well. Add 3 eggs, one at a time, blending well. Add egg yolk, pumpkin pie filling, cinnamon, nutmeg and flour, mixing well. Pour filling into form pan, atop crust, and bake at 375 degrees for 25 minutes. Reduce oven to 325 degrees and bake for an additional one hour. While baking, make topping by combining in a mixing bowl, brown sugar, flour, and softened butter, mixing well. Remove cheesecake from oven, add topping and return to oven to bake for 20 minutes or until set. Cool for one hour, then refrigerate a minimum of 8 hours before serving.

219

Chocolate Crepes with Kahlua Sauce

Yield   28 Servings

Ingredients

	Ice Cream Δ
	Parchment Paper

Crepes
1⅓ Cups	Flour
4	Eggs
1 Cup	Water
⅔ Cup	Milk
3 Tbls	Butter - softened
9 tsp	Sugar
1 Tbl	Cocoa Powder
2 tsp	Vanilla
½ tsp	Salt

Kahlua Sauce
1 Lb	Unsweetened Chocolate - chopped
2½ Cups	Light Corn Syrup
1⅔ Cups	Sugar
1¼ Cups	Butter - softened
10 Tbls	Milk
5 Tbls	Vanilla
½ Cup	Kahlua

Whipped Cream
2 Cups	Heavy Cream
1 tsp	Vanilla
1 tsp	Powdered Sugar
	Fresh Mint Leaves

Cooks Notes

PREPARATION

Place a mixing bowl in freezer to chill in preparation for making whipped cream. Cut parchment paper into 10 inch squares. Prepare ice cream rolls by placing ¾ cup ice cream on a piece of parchment paper and working the ice cream into a tube shaped roll about 6 inches long. Roll ice cream in parchment paper, twisting ends of paper to seal ends of roll, and place in freezer to firm up.

Prepare crepe batter by combining in a mixing bowl, flour, eggs, water, milk, softened butter, sugar, cocoa powder, vanilla and salt, mixing well. Allow batter to stand for 30 minutes before cooking crepes. Cook crepes in a crepe pan, or small, non-stick, small sauté pan. Preheat pan until pan is hot, place 2 Tbls of crepe batter in center of pan, tilt pan to cover entire inner surface of pan with thin layer of batter. Cook crepe until firm and loose in pan. Cooked crepe should fall freely from pan when pan is inverted. In turn, cook additional crepes until all batter is used.

Prepare Kahlua sauce by heating in a double boiler, over low heat, unsweetened chocolate bits, corn syrup, sugar, and softened butter, heating until chocolate is melted and mixture is smooth. Remove from heat, add milk, vanilla and Kahlua, stirring well.

Prepare whipped cream by placing heavy cream, vanilla and powdered sugar in small mixing bowl chilled in freezer, and whipping until a stiff peak forms.

Assemble dessert by removing ice cream roll from parchment paper, placing ice cream roll in center of crepe, and wrapping crepe around ice cream roll. Place one or two wrapped rolls on a dessert plate, top each roll with 2 Tbls Kahlua sauce, a dollop of whipped cream, and garnish with a fresh mint leaf.

HINTS

Δ Any ice cream may be used: vanilla and chocolate are the favorites at the Inn.

CHOCOLATE RASPBERRY CHEESECAKE

YIELD   ONE CHEESECAKE

INGREDIENTS

Crust
| 1½ Cups | Chocolate Cookies - finely crushed |
| 2 Tbls | Margarine - melted |

Raspberry Sauce
| 6 oz | IQF Raspberries |
| ½ Cup | Sugar |

Batter
1½ Lbs	Cream Cheese - softened
⅝ Cup	Sugar
2	Eggs
½ Cup	Sour Cream
½ tsp	Vanilla
½ Cup	Semisweet Chocolate Morsels - melted

Topping
| ¾ Cup | Semisweet Chocolate Pieces |
| ¼ Cup | Heavy Cream |

Whipped Cream
¾ Cup	Heavy Cream
½ tsp	Vanilla
1 tsp	Powdered Sugar

Cooks Notes

PREPARATION

Place a mixing bowl in freezer to chill in preparation for making whipped cream. Prepare crust by combining, in a mixing bowl, crushed cookies and margarine, mixing well by hand. Press mixture into a 9½ inch spring form pan, covering bottom and up the sides ¼ inch.

Prepare Raspberry Sauce by combining, in a blender, thawed raspberries and sugar, blending to a puree.

Begin preparation of batter by preheating oven to 325 degrees. Melt ½ cup semisweet chocolate morsels in double boiler and set aside for use in batter. Make batter by combining 1 Lb softened cream cheese and sugar in mixing bowl, mixing well until blended. Add eggs one at a time, mixing well after each, then blend in sour cream and vanilla, mixing well. Pour mixture into form pan, over crust. In a separate mixing bowl, combine remaining softened cream cheese and melted chocolate, mixing until well blended. Add ¼ of the raspberry sauce, mix well. Drop rounded tablespoonfuls of this chocolate cheesecake batter on top of the plain cheesecake batter already in the form pan. Do not swirl in. Bake at 325 degrees for 80 minutes. Remove from oven, loosen cake from the side of springform pan, allow to cool before removing side of pan.

Prepare topping by melting chocolate morsels in a double boiler over low heat then adding heavy cream and stirring until smooth. Chill topping for at least 30 minutes, then spread topping over cooled cheesecake.

Prepare whipped cream by placing heavy cream, vanilla and powdered sugar in small mixing bowl chilled in freezer, whip until stiff peak. To serve, place on a dessert plate 1 - 2 Tbls Raspberry Sauce, and rest a slice of Chocolate Raspberry Cheesecake atop the Sauce, then top with a dollop of whipped cream.

223

Chocolate Raspberry Brownies

Yield   12 Servings

Cooks Notes

Ingredients

Brownie

4 oz	Unsweetened Chocolate
½ Cup	Margarine
1¾ Cups	Sugar - granulated
3	Eggs
1½ tsp	Vanilla
¼ tsp	Salt
1 Cup	Flour
3 oz	IQF Raspberries ◊1
2 Tbls	Butter - softened
2 Tbls	Corn Syrup
1 Cup	Powdered Sugar
1 Tbl	Milk
1 tsp	Vanilla

Preparation

Prepare brownies by melting over medium to low heat in a double boiler, 3 oz chocolate and margarine. Add 1½ cups granulated sugar. Preheat oven to 325 degrees. In a mixing bowl, blend together eggs, vanilla, and salt, then add the chocolate mixture and mix well. Add flour and mix well ◊2. Pour batter into a greased 8 inch square pan and bake at 325 degrees for 40 minutes. While brownies are baking, make raspberry sauce by combining, in a blender, thawed raspberries and ¼ cup granulated sugar, blending to a puree. Remove brownies from oven and spread raspberry sauce over the entire top of pan of brownies, then cool. Make frosting by melting, in a sauce pan, remaining chocolate and blending in softened butter and corn syrup. Then stir in powdered sugar, milk and vanilla, mixing well. After brownies have cooled, spread frosting over top of raspberry sauce.

Variations

◊1 Strawberries or cherries may be substituted for the raspberries, to add a different fruit flavor to the brownies.
◊2 To make Walnut Brownies, add ½ cup walnut pieces to batter before baking.

HEAVENLY ANGEL PIE ♣

YIELD   ONE PIE

INGREDIENTS   *Cooks Notes*

6	Eggs
1½ Cups	Sugar
½ tsp	Cream of Tartar
4 Tbls	Lemon Juice
1 Tbl	Lemon Peel - grated
⅛ tsp	Salt
2 Cups	Heavy Cream

PREPARATION

Separate eggs, reserving whites from four of the eggs, and
yolks from all six. Allow reserved whites to warm to room
temperature. Place a mixing bowl in freezer to chill in
preparation for making whipped cream. Preheat oven to
250 degrees. In a mixing bowl, prepare meringue by
beating egg whites until stiff. Slowly add 1 cup sugar and
cream of tartar. Continue to beat several minutes until
glossy and stiff. Pour into 10 inch greased pyrex pie plate,
pushing beaten egg whites high up on sides of pie plate,
forming a pie shell. Bake at 250 degrees for one hour.
Turn off oven and cool meringue shell in oven with the
door opened a crack until oven has completely cooled,
about one hour.

In the top of a double boiler, prepare filling by beating
egg yolks until lemon colored. Add remaining sugar,
lemon juice, lemon peel and salt. Cook in double boiler
until mixture thickens, about 8 - 10 minutes. Cool. In the
chilled mixing bowl, whip cream until it peaks. Blend ½
of whipped cream into cooled lemon mixture. Pour lemon
filling into cooled meringue shell, chill filled pie in
refrigerator until fillings has firmed, about 2 hours, then
spread the remainder of the whipped cream over pie. Chill
24 hours before serving.

CHOCOLATE PEANUT BUTTER ICE CREAM PIE ♣

YIELD   ONE PIE

INGREDIENTS

3 Qts	Chocolate Ice Cream
½ Cup	Dry Roasted Peanuts - finely chopped
9 Inch	Chocolate Pie Shell
7	Miniature Peanut Butter Cups - quartered

Kahlua Sauce
1 Lb	Unsweetened Chocolate - chopped
2½ Cups	Light Corn Syrup
1⅔ Cups	Sugar - granulated
1¼ Cups	Butter - softened
10 Tbls	Milk
5 Tbls	Vanilla
½ Cup	Kahlua

Whipped Cream
¾ Cup	Heavy Cream
½ tsp	Vanilla
1 tsp	Powdered Sugar

CREAM

COMASI DAIRY
1 PINT

Cooks Notes

PREPARATION

Soften ice cream by removing from freezer and by placing
in refrigerator for about 20 minutes. Finely chop peanuts
in a food processor. Press chopped peanuts into the base
of the pie crust, then sprinkle on ½ cup of the quartered
peanut butter cups. In a mixing bowl combine softened
ice cream and remaining quartered peanut butter cups,
mixing well, then place mixture in prepared pie crust,
over quartered peanut butter cups and chopped peanuts.
Round top, cover with plastic wrap, and freeze overnight.
Prepare Kahlua Sauce by heating in a double boiler, over
low heat, unsweetened chocolate bits, corn syrup, granulated sugar, and softened butter, heating until chocolate is
melted and mixture is smooth. Remove from heat, add
milk, vanilla and Kahlua, stirring well.

Before serving, prepare whipped cream by chilling mixing
bowl in freezer for at least one hour, then whipping heavy
cream, vanilla and powdered sugar in chilled bowl until
stiff.

Allow pie to soften by holding at room temperature for
10 - 15 minutes before cutting slices. Serve each slice of
pie on a dessert plate, topped with 2 Tbls of Kahlua Sauce
and a dollop of whipped cream.

PECAN PRALINE CHEESECAKE WITH BUTTERSCOTCH SAUCE ♣

YIELD   ONE CHEESECAKE

INGREDIENTS

Crust
1½ Cups	Graham Cracker Crumbs
2 Tbls	Sugar - granulated
¼ Cup	Pecans - finely chopped
4 Tbls	Butter - melted

Batter
1 Cup	Pecans - chopped
3 Tbls	Butter - softened
1½ Lbs	Cream Cheese - softened
1 Cup	Dark Brown Sugar
1 tsp	Vanilla
2 Tbls	Flour
3	Eggs

Topping
1½ tsp	Sugar - granulated
¼ Cup	Dark Brown Sugar
2 Tbls	Heavy Cream
1 Tbl	Butter - softened
½ tsp	Vanilla

Butterscotch Sauce
6 Tbls	Butter - softened
1 Cup	Dark Brown Sugar
⅔ Cup	Heavy Cream
1 tsp	Vanilla

PREPARATION

Prepare crust by combining, in a mixing bowl, graham cracker crumbs, sugar, chopped pecans and melted butter, mixing well. Pat crust into the base of a 9½ inch spring form pan coming up the sides about ¼ inch. Preheat oven to 350 degrees.

Prepare batter, by first making praline chunks. Combine chopped pecans and softened butter, mixing well. Spread mixture evenly on a baking pan and bake at 350 degrees until golden brown, about 5 minutes. Be careful not to burn. Remove from oven, cool, and break into ½ inch chunks. Reduce oven temperature to 325 degrees. In a large mixing bowl, combine softened cream cheese, brown sugar, vanilla and flour, mixing well. Add eggs, one at a time, mixing well. Then add cooled praline chunks, reserving ¼ cup of the chunks. Pour batter into spring form pan, filling crust, and bake at 325 degrees for 60 minutes. After 60 minutes turn oven off and allow cheesecake to cool in the closed oven for thirty minutes. Then remove from oven, loosen spring form pan and remove sides, then allow to cool to room temperature.

Prepare topping by combining, in a sauté pan, granulated sugar, brown sugar, heavy cream and softened butter, mixing well. Cook on medium to high heat until sugars have dissolved and mixture is at soft ball stage (250 degrees on a candy thermometer). Remove from heat and cool slightly, then add vanilla and stir until creamy. Top cooled baked cheesecake with remaining pecan chunks. Then pour the topping over chunks. Refrigerate at least 8 hours before serving.

Prepare Butterscotch Sauce by melting butter in a sauté pan. Add brown sugar and heavy cream and bring to a boil. Boil for 5 minutes without stirring. Remove sauce from heat and add vanilla. Cool to room temperature. To serve cheesecake, place each piece of cheesecake on a dessert plate and top each with 2 Tbls Butterscotch Sauce.

Strawberry Cheesecake

Yield   One Cheesecake

Ingredients

Crust
2	Lemons - zest only
½ Cup	Flour
1 Cup	Powdered Sugar
1	Egg Yolk
½ Cup	Butter - softened

Batter
2 Lbs	Cream Cheese - softened
1½ Cups	Sugar - granulated
4	Eggs
2	Egg Yolks
2 Tbls	Flour
2 tsp	Vanilla
1 Cup	Fresh Strawberries - blended

Topping
1 Cup	Sour Cream
1 Tbl	Sugar - granulated
1 tsp	Vanilla

Whipped Cream
¾ Cup	Heavy Cream
½ tsp	Vanilla
1 tsp	Powdered Sugar
12	Fresh Strawberries - sliced

Cooks Notes

PREPARATION

Prepare crust by combining, in a mixing bowl, lemon zest,
½ cup flour, powdered sugar, 1 egg yolk and softened
butter, mixing well. Place in a 9½ inch spring form pan,
patting the crust in the base of the pan and up the sides
about ¼ inch.

Preheat oven to 400 degrees. Prepare batter by combining
in a mixing bowl, softened cream cheese and 1 cup
granulated sugar, mixing well. Add eggs, one at a time,
mixing well. Add egg yolks, one at a time, mixing well.
Add flour and vanilla, mixing well. Add blended strawberries and ½ cup granulated sugar, mixing well. Pour batter
into the prepared form pan, filling crust and bake at 400
degrees for 15 minutes. Reduce oven temperature to 300
degrees and bake an additional one hour.

While baking, prepare topping by combining in a mixing
bowl, sour cream, granulated sugar and vanilla, mixing
well by hand. After cheesecake has baked a total of 75
minutes pour topping on cheesecake and bake an additional 15 minutes. Remove from oven and cool for 30
minutes. Then refrigerate at least 8 hours before serving.
Before serving, prepare whipped cream by chilling mixing
bowl in freezer for at least one hour, then whipping heavy
cream, vanilla and powdered sugar in chilled bowl until
stiff. Serve each slice of cheesecake by topping with a
dollop of whipped cream and a sliced fresh strawberry.

INDEX

Front Cover Photograph by Jim Rantala, Traverse City, Michigan
Back Cover Photograph by Glen Petersen, Petersen Productions, Traverse City,
Michigan

Title Page Illustration by Lyn Boyer-Pennington, Traverse City, Michigan
Interior Illustrations by Peggy Core, Suttons Bay, Michigan

Cover Design by Jim DeWildt, Traverse City, Michigan
Interior Design by Peggy Core & Jim DeWildt

Proofreading by Virginia & Frank Sisson

Printed by McNaughton & Gunn, Saline, Michigan

Printed on Recycled Paper

The text was set in Adobe Garamond type. All illustrations were digitized by
Adobe Photoshop and placed electronically. Layout was done on an Apple
Macintosh Quadra 610 using Aldus Pagemaker and film was output on a
Linotronic 530.

Additional copies of this book are available
for $19.95 plus $3.50 for postage and handling.
(Canadian Orders $24.95 CDN plus $4.00)

By mail:
The Leelanau Country Inn
149 East Harbor Highway
Maple City, MI 49664

Or, by telephone from 9 am to 5 pm:
800 - COOK 441

American Express - VISA - MasterCard

Volume purchase discounts available.

For Trade Orders Please Contact:

Publishers Distribution Service
6893 Sullivan Road
Grawn, MI 49637
Voice: 800 - 345 - 0096
FAX: 800 - 950 - 9793

PUBLISHERS
DISTRIBUTION
S E R V I C E